Herbs of the Northern Shaman

A Guide to Mind-Altering
Plants of the
Northern Hemisphere

Herbs of the Northern Shaman

A Guide to Mind-Altering Plants of the Northern Hemisphere

Steve Andrews
and Katrinia Rindsberg

BOOKS

Winchester, UK
Washington, USA

First published by O-Books, 2010
O-Books is an imprint of John Hunt Publishing Ltd., Laurel House, Station Approach,
Alresford, Hants, SO24 9JH, UK
office1@o-books.net
www.o-books.com

For distributor details and how to order please visit the 'Ordering' section on our website.

ISBN: 978 1 84694 369 0

Design: Stuart Davies

Printed and bound by CPI Group (UK) Ltd, Croydon, CR0 4YY

Neither the authors nor the publisher assumes any responsibility for the use or misuse of
information contained in this book. It is sold for entertainment purposes only.
Be Warned!

Photos and Illustrations by Katrinia Rindsberg

Cover by Ole Rindsberg

We operate a distinctive and ethical publishing philosophy in all
areas of our business, from our global network of authors to
production and worldwide distribution.

CONTENTS

Foreword   1

Alphabetical Listing   4
Asafetida   4
Asarabacca   5
Bearberry   7
Big Laughing Gym   8
Bittersweet   9
Broom (Scotch)   11
Bugleweed   12
Burdock   13
Buttercup (Meadow)   15
Calamus   16
California Poppy   19
Cannabis   20
Catnip   26
Cinquefoil   27
Columbine   29
Common Reed   31
Corydalis   31
Damiana   32
Deadly Nightshade   33
Dogwood   36
Doñana   37
Ergot   38
Fennel   40
Fly Agaric   41
Fumitory   44
Galangal   46
Hawkweed   47
Hellebore (Black)   49
Hemlock   51
Henbane   53

Hops 55
Japanese Belladonna 57
Juniper 58
Labrador Tea 60
Lime (Large-leaved) 61
Lobelia 62
Magic Mushrooms 64
Mandrake 70
Mistletoe 73
Monkshood 76
Mormon Tea 78
Morning Glory 79
Motherwort 82
Opium Poppy 84
Passion Flower 87
Pennyroyal 88
Periwinkle 90
Peyote 92
Phalaris Grasses 99
Phytolacca 101
Prairie Mimosa 103
Rhododendron 104
Saffron 105
Saint John's Wort 108
Sassafras 109
Skullcap 111
Strawberry Tree 113
Syrian Rue 114
Thorn Apple 116
Tobacco 119
Valerian 122
Vervain 124
Water Lily (White) 126
Wild Lettuce 128
Woodruff 130
Woolly Yarrow 132

Wormwood   133
Yaupon   135

Books and Literature Consulted in Researching this Material   137
Botanical Glossary   139
Glossary of Medical Terms   141
Index   148

A nicely produced reference book for anyone interested in the use of psychoactive herbs. The herbs covered range from the obvious ones such as Fly Agaric, Magic Mushrooms, Mandrake, Thorn Apple and Vervain to more obscure herbs like corydalis, hawkweed, periwinkle and saffron, to name but a few.

Witchcraft & Wicca, Avalonia,
http://ritualmagick.co.uk/reviews/?tag=shamanism

The writer is clearly an expert in several fields, being not only an informed naturalist, an inspired horticulturalist and experimenter with odd additions to his house-plant collection, but a mystic traveller too. One feels a certain confidence in his sure-footed guidance around this obscure but fascinating area of knowledge.

So whether you merely wish to browse on the subject of alchemical gardening, or prefer to experiment with free and freely available mind-altering substances, this book is a must for you. Highly recommended.

CJ Stone.

As someone with a general interest in plants and herbs I thoroughly enjoyed reading this book, it is easy to read and well presented and contains a lot of information which is new to me. I found it fascinating and friendly at the same time and would recommend it to any with an interest in flora.

Carrie de Fey, From http://www.warband.org/review_herbs.html

This really is an excellent book. I own a copy, and I would definitely recommend it. It includes many many entries, not only the usual suspects, but also many plants you will find growing wild in Europe and America. It contains information about the recreational, entheogenic, medicinal and magical use of plants. Highly recommended.

Plot55, http://www.plot55.com/books/herbs_shaman.html

If anyone can locate mind altering northern hemisphere plants then it's the bard of Ely (Cardiff) Steve Andrews. This easy to read, well illustrated and informative directory is about as comprehensive as you can get - how do you want your mind altered? How much do you want to pay? What risks do you run? is it illegal? Where do the plants grow? Can you nurture them yourself out the back? Steve does, shows how, explains and entertains. A must.

Peter Finch

Whether you are a retired hippy now paying rent on a residential caravan, a beach bum with a time share in Ibiza or simply a traveller seeking to catalogue the wonders of this ephemeral planet, take a look inside Steve's magic collection to expand your awareness of what is out there.

Robert Parker-Munn

Herbs Of The Northern Shaman is very strongly recommended reading for students of botany and natural hallucinogens, as well as personal and academic psychoactive plants reference collections.

Midwest Book Review, Oregon, WI USA

Dedication

Dedicated to all shamans of the world and to everyone with an open mind. We have all the tools we need for exploration, for healing and for magic. Let's use them with wisdom as we enter the new Age of Aquarius.

Acknowledgements

Herbs of the Northern Shaman was originally published in 2000 by Loompanics Unlimited but sadly that company has had to close down and my book went out of print. Due to ongoing public interest and demand for this work it is being resurrected on O-Books with some changes, and the help of my good friend Katrinia Rindsberg, whose beautiful photography will grace the pages and replace the original illustrations and photos.

Thanks are due to all the authors and researchers whose work I have consulted and to all the shamans who experienced for themselves and for their tribes, some of the things I have described. Additional thanks to authors C.J. Stone and Richard Rudgley, and to Louise McNamara of Thorsons book company, for their encouragement and support with the original version.

Especial gratitude goes to Gia, Mike and all at Loompanics for publishing the first edition of Herbs of the Northern Shaman and in helping me make known some of the knowledge of our plant teachers.

Foreword

Throughout history and continuing onward from the present day, a very wide range of trees, plants and fungi have been used, for a multitude of purposes wherever people have lived. Many herbs are used for culinary reasons, many others as medicinal cures and preventative tonics and many more for all of these purposes. Throughout the world, an extensive number have been in widespread usage because of the mind-altering properties they possess. Lots of these have been recognised as magical plants and used by practitioners of tribal shamanism, witchcraft and other esoteric practices.

The ancient Druids of Britain as well as the Nordic shamans of Scandinavia and Russia are known to have used many of these herbs and it can be easily conjectured that these plants played a big part in their sacred knowledge and rituals. The Native American tribes have a long history of using such herbal preparations too, and many of these psychoactive plants have been experimented with and employed by the new psychedelic generations. In macrobiotic philosophy it is believed that food plants are tailored to the needs of people living in a specific region, so might it not also be the case that psychoactive herbs follow a similar design? In other words, to contact elemental and nature spirits or to be in tune with the environment, might not local vision-inducing herbs be the best ones to choose?

This book is intended as a guide to mind-altering plants that have the potential for shamanic use and that grow wild in the Northern Hemisphere. The planetary rulers and associated deities for each herb are listed, where known, for anyone interested in this information.

Plants that affect the mental state of the consumer have found their way into the cultures and sub-cultures of the world's populations and civilisations. They have played a large role in folklore and myth and have always been employed by those who seek knowledge of the nature and laws of the non-physical and spiritual realms.

Their power to move the minds of users can inspire creative artistry, spiritual understanding and religious imagery or act by motivating the darker side of human consciousness with visions of horror and

1

insanity.

Many such plants are used as medicines as well as for their mental effects and there is an exceedingly slim line between beneficial tonic or cure and a toxic poison in very many cases.

Today and throughout the ages, a large group of people have sought to make use of herbal preparations for the drugs contained in them, as a recreational escape from the pressures of life, for pleasure and pure Hedonism, or for an exploration of the deeper mysteries of life.

We all are well aware of the dangers of drug abuse and the continuing debate on the legal status of many herbs and their extracts but this book does not wish to take sides and enter that area of discussion. Rather, it is intended as a concise guide and an educational text for anyone seeking further knowledge of the magic of the plant kingdoms. The author wishes to make it clear that he is not condoning or advocating the experimentation with or usage of such herbs. A word of warning will be included with all plants in this work that are known to be of a very dangerous and poisonous nature.

Some plants act as stimulants, some have calming or sedative effects, others are narcotic painkillers, whilst yet more have hallucinogenic or psychedelic properties. There are plants that exhibit several of these qualities depending on dosage taken.

The plants listed and described in this book have either been used for one or more of these effects or contain substances that can provoke such reactions and are, therefore, included for this reason and as a matter of interest.

Many shamanic herbs face danger of extinction in the wild, due in the main to the on-going destruction of natural habitats as well as the attention of over-zealous plant-collectors. Some people are helping to conserve species by cultivating them domestically and passing stock on to others as well as re-introducing the plants back into the wild. Whilst such efforts are to be highly commended it must be pointed out that taking wild plants from their habitats can add further to their decline, and in many places is illegal. Anyone wishing to aid the conservation of such herbs is, therefore, advised to contact a reputable supplier of domestically cultivated seeds and plants. Many species are available from nurseries and general horticultural suppliers but more specialised varieties and rarities can also be purchased from companies that specialise in stocking these plants.

There already exists a huge catalogue of books and literature about the psychoactive plants of the world but, as yet, there is no such work devoted only to those found growing in the Northern Hemisphere. I hope in this volume to remedy this and to reveal a bit more about the mysteries of these sacred herbs and plant-teachers.

Disclaimer

Finally, for legal reasons, I must include the following disclaimer: Whilst every care has been observed in researching and writing this book, the publishers and their representatives cannot accept any responsibility for any damage or harm resulting from advice, infor-mation or treatment stemming from this work.

Steve Andrews

A

Asafetida
Umbelliferae
Ferula foetida
Other names: Asafoetida, Devil's Dung, Gum Asafetida, Food of the Gods, Hing

The Asafetida is a very tall herb from the Parsley family that comes from Afghanistan and Persia, where it grows in the mountains. It has been successfully cultivated in the Edinburgh Botanical Gardens, where it reaches between six and ten foot in height. It was first discovered in a sandy desert of Aral in 1844 but has been actually known since the 12th century.

In Afghanistan it is found growing indigenously from two to four thousand feet above sea level and in these high plains where it is found the conditions are usually very arid in winter but are transformed by a luxuriant growth of this herb in summer. It bears huge folded cabbage-like flower heads, which are eaten raw by the native people there.

The flowers are a greenish-yellow or pale whitish and are carried in large umbels. The whole plant has an offensive odour similar to garlic and is full of a milky sap, which is strong smelling and very bitter to taste. Asafetida has a large fleshy root covered in bristly fibres and a good source of this resinous liquid. This latex-like juice is the source of the drug or condiment known in Asia as hing.

Four-year old plants that haven't yet flowered have their roots exposed and slashed. These roots are then shaded from the sun and left for five or six weeks for the gummy resin to leak out and solidify. The hardened gum is broken into lumps of a reddish colour and these are placed in leather bags and sent off to markets. To add to the bulk weight, along the way, it is frequently adulterated with all manner of matter ranging from inferior quality Asafetida through to red clay, sand and stones. A particularly fine grade of Asafetida is sold in Indian bazaars as "Kandaharre Hing".

In India it has been long-employed in medicine and also in cookery. Asafetida is a stimulant, an antispasmodic and an expectorant. It has been used successfully to treat convulsions, hysteria, croup, asthma, bronchitis and whooping cough. Also Asafetida has been prescribed for cases of stomach irritation and colic. It is an excellent laxative as well. Because of the bitter taste it is usually consumed medicinally as a pill. It contains oleo-gum-resin and ferulic acid. The strong smell and flavour is caused by the volatile oil in it. Despite the unpleasant odour and flavour of the herb it is a staple part of Eastern cuisine and is included in many recipes for curry and other sauces.

Asafetida is ruled by Saturn and associated with the deities Athene and Priapus.

Asarabacca
Aristolochiaceae
Asarum europaeum
Other names: Hazel-wort, Wild Ginger, Wild Nard

Asarabacca is an evergreen creeping herb, which grows in woodlands, although it is rarely encountered in the UK. It grows more commonly in parts of Europe and as far north as Finland. It is rather an unusual looking plant with short stems up to four inches tall, bearing kidney-shaped deep green leaves and solitary dark purplish flowers.

Although I cannot trace any use of this plant for mind-altering purposes as such, it does contain variable amounts of asarone, which is a substance also found in Calamus, a species used for its stimulant and hallucinogenic properties. Calamus is employed in magical rituals and is covered later on in this book.

Asarabacca has been used, albeit rarely, as a medicinal herb for liver complaints, laryngitis, asthma, bronchitis and dropsy, but it is not recommended because of harmful side effects. This herb is a purgative and diuretic as well as having emetic and stimulant properties and it is reported that drunkards in France have used the herb to induce vomiting. Powdered Asarabacca has been used in snuff. When being used for medicinal purposes the entire plant is first gathered and then dried in a warm place. Active constituents: asarone, essential oil, resins, mucilage and flavonoids.

Asarabacca is a herb of Mars.

B

Bearberry
Ericaceae
Arctostaphylos uva-ursi

Other names: Arberry, Bear's Grape, Burren Myrtle, Dogberry,
Kinnikinnick, Mealberry, Moanague, Mountain Box, Red Bearberry,
Rockberry, Sagackhomi, Upland Cranberry, Uva-ursi

This is an evergreen shrub that grows on the mountains and moors of
Europe, North America and Canada, northern Asia and in Japan.

Many of the Northwest Indian tribes, such as the Ojibway, used this
in their shamanic smoking mixtures for its inebriating effects. Not
surprisingly its totem beast is the bear.

Bearberry has been used medicinally as a diuretic and astringent
and for treating kidney, bladder and urinary tract disorders. It was
favoured in the 13th century by the Welsh physicians and has been
included in many proprietary medicines since then, including lots of
herbal remedies that are available today. A word of caution, however,
needs to be added, as it should only be used for short periods of time,
preferably under the supervision of a qualified medical practitioner or

herbalist. Otherwise it can cause vomiting, nausea and more serious poisoning. Bearberry contains arbutin, ericolin, gallic, malic and ursolic acids, quercetin, hydroquinolone, volatile oil, essential oils and tannin. Bearberry is a herb ruled by the planets Mars and Pluto.

Big Laughing Gym
Cortinariaceae
Gymnopilus spectabilis/ Gymnopilus junonius
Other names: Big Laughing Jim, Laughing Jim, Laughing Mushroom, Waraitake

Big Laughing Gym is a widely distributed psychoactive mushroom that is found growing in clusters on decaying trees such as conifers and deciduous stumps and logs, or on the ground from buried wood, from early summer through until the first frosts.

Big Laughing Gym contains varying amounts of psilocin and psilocybin, which cause the hallucinogenic intoxication this fungus can produce. In Japan, where it is known as "Waraitake", which means "laughing mushroom", it was said to have caused a group of Buddhist nuns and priests, who ate some of this fungus in error, to have gone laughing and dancing around a town. The cap of Big Laughing Gym ranges from 7 to 42 centimetres across, is convex, and is bright orange, orange-brown or a reddish-brown and with a dry scaly surface. It has a rusty orange spore print, a bitter taste, stains red with potassium hydroxide and turns green when cooked in a pan.

It is said that specimens of Big Laughing Gym from the eastern parts of North America or Japan are more likely to contain psilocybin than similar mushrooms found in the western part of the US or in Europe.

Because of the possibility of mistaking Big Laughing Gym for other dangerous species of woodland mushroom it is wise not to consume any without positive identification by a fungus expert.

Bittersweet
Solanaceae
Solanum Dulcamara
Other names: Dulcamara, Felonwood, Felonwort, Scarlet Berry, Violet Bloom, Woody Nightshade

The Bittersweet is a very common climbing perennial from the Potato and Nightshade family and is found throughout North America, Canada and Europe. It grows in hedges, waste-places, railway banks and even in swamps and at the edge of water. Where other bushes and plants support it its trailing stems reach several feet in length.

Bittersweet has auriculate leaves on the upper parts of its stems and heart-shaped foliage below. The stems are green and slightly hairy at first but become woody with age, hence one of its common names. The Bittersweet has small purple starry flowers borne in clusters and followed by scarlet-red berries.

Bittersweet produces its flowers from July onwards and is a conspicuous sight in our hedgerows. It is often mistaken for its far more dangerous relative the Deadly Nightshade, although the leaves, flowers and berries are very different and much smaller. The Deadly Nightshade is a far more uncommon plant than its woody cousin the Bittersweet.

In America there is yet another plant, which is confused with the

Bittersweet, namely, the American Bittersweet or Waxwork (*Celastrus scandens*). This plant is also called False Bittersweet and is very different in appearance and therapeutic action, besides belonging to another family of plants.

Bittersweet, like so many other herbs in this very large Solanacae family, is a narcotic. The twigs and root-bark are the parts harvested and have a taste that is sweet at first and then becoming bitter, as its name so aptly suggests.

Bittersweet is used to treat skin diseases, bronchial conditions, whooping cough and asthma, as well as rheumatic complaints. Besides being a narcotic it also increases bodily secretions and has expectorant and diuretic properties. Bittersweet contains the alkaloid solanine and the glucoside dulcamarine. The former of these substances acts as a narcotic and in large doses it paralyses the central nervous system, causing vertigo, delerium and convulsions. It can slow breathing and cardiac function leading to heart failure and death.

Although it is a lot weaker in its effects than Deadly Nightshade it can still prove capable of the same lethal consequences. Unlike its dangerous relative the Deadly Nightshade, Bittersweet has no effect on the pupils of the eye and causes no dilation.

Culpeper said of the herb Bittersweet: "It is good to remove witch-craft both in men and beast and all sudden diseases whatsoever." This is interesting information indeed, considering that witches, as an essential part of their "craft", use many of the other herbs in its family.

Bittersweet is a herb under the dominion of Mercury.

Broom (Scotch)
Papilionaceae /Leguminosae
Cytisus scoparius
Other names: Basam, Bisom, Bizzom, Breeam, Browme, Brum, Green Broom

The Scotch Broom is an attractive yellow-flowered shrub frequently found growing on hillsides, heaths, sand dunes, waste places and in open woodland throughout the countryside. It is often cultivated in parks and gardens too. Broom is found throughout northern Europe and Asia and is naturalised in North America.

Medicinally, Broom is a diuretic and also has the effect of dilating the blood vessels. Cytisine, one of the alkaloids it contains, can be very toxic, having a similar effect to digitalis, the heart drug extracted from

Foxgloves (*Digitalis purpurea*). It is therefore not recommended for internal ingestion in any form unless under medical supervision.

Broom also contains sparteine, genisteine, hydroxytyramine, scaparin, bitter principles and essential oil. When smoked, in the form of dried Broom flowers that have been stored and aged in a sealed jar for ten days, these substances can produce a relaxed high.

The Spanish Broom *(Spartium junceum)* has been also used for similar purposes and so has the Canary Island Broom (*Genista canariensis*). Apparently the latter species of Broom was introduced into Mexico and found favour with the Yaqui Indian shamans there.

The Broom has always been a traditional tool for sweeping clean, and the broomstick, of course, is associated with witches, besides being used for domestic purposes.

Bugleweed
Labiatae
Lycopus virginicus
Other names: Gipsyweed, Gipsywort, Sweet Bugle, Water Bugle, Water Horehound

The Bugleweed is a common weed of damp and shady ground in the eastern parts of North America. Like its European cousin the Bugle (*Ajuga reptans*) it belongs to the same family of plants and herbs, which includes the Mint and the Sage. Unlike its European relative it is in a different genus. Again, like the Bugle, it is a perennial creeping plant and Bugleweed bears purple flowers on fairly short flowering spikes, although it can reach nearly 2 feet in height. It is in flower from July to September and the herb has a pleasant aroma a bit like Mint.

Bugleweed can be dried for infusions or used fresh and is a treatment for coughs, consumption and bronchial problems. It contains a bitter principle and lycopin. Bugleweed has astringent properties. Bugleweed can also be used as a sedative and mild narcotic.

<h1 style="text-align:center">Burdock</h1>

Compositae

Arctium lappa

Other names: Bardana, Bardona, Bazzies, Beggar's Buttons, Cockle-bur plant, Cockle Buttons, Clite, Clog-weed, Clot-Bur, Cloud Burr, Cuckold Buttons, Cuckoo Button, Donkeys, Edible Burdock, Eddick, Flapper-bags, Fox's Clote, Great Burdock, Gypsy Comb, Happy Major, Hardock, Hurr-burr, Kisses, Loppy Major, Love Leaves, Personata, Pig's Rhubarb, Sweethearts, Sticky Jacks, Thorny Burr, Touch-me-not, Turkey Burrseed, Tuzzy-muzzy, Wild Rhubarb

The Burdock is a plant known to everyone from their childhood as something that goes into "Dandelion and Burdock" pop and as the source of the sticky burs, so ideal for throwing at playmates.

Burdock is a fairly tall biennial herb that grows on waste ground, roadsides, in woodlands and on banks and grassy places throughout Europe, Asia and North America.

The whole plant, including the roots and seeds, are collected, dried and used in herbal medicine as a blood-purifier, against colds and fevers, for skin diseases such as eczema and Burdock is one of the herbs that go into the "Essiac" Native American cancer cure formula. Burdock contains arctiin, inulin, tannins and volatile oil as its active constituents. It is also thought highly of in oriental macrobiotics, where, like Ginseng, Burdock is regarded as a yang herb.

Doctor H. Winter Griffith, describing Burdock, states in the Vitamin Fact File (herbal section) "it may be contaminated by atropine like chemicals that can be poisonous," and that "hallucinations" may be caused. For this reason I have included Burdock here as a potential shamanic herb.

However, since the first edition of this book was published further evidence has come to light suggesting that Burdock does not contain atropine. Many websites such as this one - http://www.herbs2000.com/herbs/herbs_Burdock.htm - explain that the reported cases involving symptoms of poisoning, which had been thought to have been caused by the consumption of Burdock tea, were later shown to have been caused by contamination of the Burdock root in the tea with Belladonna root, which does contain atropine.

In other words Burdock root itself is harmless but if it is contaminated with Belladonna root as an adulterant then it is not. It would therefore be wise when using Burdock root to be careful and check the source and quality of the root before you purchase it from a supplier.

The young stalks of Burdock can be boiled like asparagus and the leaves eaten in moderation as greens. Burdock root is included in the macrobiotic diet.

In magic, Burdock is regarded as a herb for protection. Burdock is associated with Blodeuwedd, the maiden who was made magically from wild flowers in the story in the Welsh Mabinogion, and it is a herb ruled by Venus.

Buttercup (Meadow)
Ranunculaceae
Ranunculus acris
Other names: Gold Cup, Grenouillette, Mao-ken, Shui-lang, Upright
Meadow Crowfoot

The common Meadow Buttercup with it shiny golden-yellow flowers is
too widely known to need much of a description, but what is not as
widely known is that it may well be a herb that can produce
psychoactive effects. According to author Gareth Rose in his booklet
The Psychedelics, early Chinese literature states that a flower that grew
by streams and brooks could cause delirium. Li Shih-chen cited
Kohung, from about 320 AD, stating that "among the herbs there is the
Shui-lang ('water-lang'- a kind of Mao-ken), a plant with rounded
leaves which grows along water courses. It is poisonous and when
eaten by mistake it produces delirium." Some authorities feel that the
herb referred to is the common species of Buttercup. Far more investigation is needed to confirm whether or not the species described
actually is the Meadow Buttercup, as the leaves of this type are not

really "rounded".

In fact, the lower leaves are variable in form but always divided and the upper leaves few in number, small and with fewer segments. If it actually is some species of Buttercup that the writings refer to then the Marsh Marigold (*Caltha palustris*) seems a more likely candidate to me as this member of the Buttercup family does have fairly rounded or kidney-shaped leaves and definitely grows alongside water.

It is, however, known for sure, that related species of Ranunculus have been used for arrow poisons and that several types contain the compound yangonin, which is an active constituent of the well-known psychoactive Kava-Kava (*Piper methysticum*), as used by Pacific Islanders for an intoxicating beverage.

The Meadow Buttercup of the species *R. acris* is known to be both toxic and so acrid that it causes inflammation and blistering. Even pulling it up and carrying it in a bare hand is reported to cause soreness of the skin the Buttercup touches. Cattle will not eat the plant but if, by chance or due to the sparseness of pasture, they do eat meadow Buttercup then they are likely to suffer blisters in their mouths.

Meadow Buttercup has been used medicinally as the juice from the leaves to treat warts, and as a plaster applied locally to ease violent headaches and gout.

With its fiery nature it comes as no surprise to learn that the Meadow Buttercup is a herb of Mars.

C

Calamus
Araceae
Acorus Calamus
Other names: Acore, Bach, Cinnamon Sedge, Gladdon, Flag Root, Myrtle Grass, Rat Root, Sweet Cane, Sweet Flag, Sweet Root, Sweet Rush, Sweet Myrtle, Sweet Sedge

The Calamus plant grows as a semi-aquatic at the edges of rivers, canals, streams, lakes and ponds as well as in marshy places in Britain, Europe, Canada and North America, Russia, China, Japan and Asia.

Calamus grows rampantly in the Norfolk Broads and can be very invasive in nature. Calamus looks similar to other flag irises and sedges hence some of its alternative names. It can be distinguished, however, by the strong aromatic smell the herb emits if lightly crushed, as well as the crinkled edges of its long spear-shaped leaves. Calamus bears a yellowish-green spike of flowers or spadix, resembling a large catkin growing the wrong way up. This flower very seldom produces seed in the UK, although the plant spreads rapidly everywhere by division of the creeping rhizome.

Calamus has a very wide range of uses in medicine, as a plant used in rituals and for its drug properties. In herbalism, Calamus is advocated for asthma, bronchitis, diarrhoea, toothache, headache, hangovers, fevers, flatulence and digestive problems, anorexia, nervous exhaustion and fatigue, and also as a remedy for gum disorders. It has been a staple of folk medicine because of its many qualities and also used as a general tonic. The dried root of Calamus has even been made into a candy.

The main active constituents of Calamus are alpha and beta asarone but it also contains acorin, choline, bitter principles, tannin, essential oil and mucilage.

The root of Calamus is harvested in spring or autumn, washed, scrubbed and dried thoroughly. It is then cut up and stored, however, it deteriorates in potency quite rapidly and will have already lost some of its properties after a few months.

Calamus is an ingredient in the recipes for "flying ointments" used by witches and also is mentioned in the Bible for use in anointing oils. In Exodus 30, verse 23 it says "and of sweet Calamus two hundred and fifty shekels," and in verse 25: "...and thou shalt make it an oil of holy ointment....it shall be an holy anointing oil." There is a further Biblical reference to the herb in Solomon 4, verse 14, where the Biblical king places the herb in his garden of delights: "Spikenard and Saffron; Calamus and cinnamon, with all trees of frankincense." Calamus is also mentioned in the books of Isaiah and Ezekiel. In Isaiah it is referred to as "sweet cane".

The Calamus root has been taken by the Cree Indians of Canada for its tonic properties as well as for its stimulant effects and has been used by other tribes to keep them alert on hunting expeditions as well as for shamanic rituals.

Calamus inspired Walt Whitman's Leaves of Grass and has thus left its mark on literature like so many shamanic herbs have also done. In fact, Whitman dedicated 39 poems to the herb - The Calamus Poems.

About 2 inches of Calamus root will produce a stimulating effect if eaten and 6 to 10 inches will cause a psychedelic experience, although the affects vary greatly from one person to the next, depending on individual levels of tolerance and quality of the herb ingested. Calamus has also been found to act as a sedative in some cases and there has been a lot of debate over its exact properties. My own experience of the herb has been as both a stimulant and a hallucinogen. I once did a twelve mile walk on Calamus with all senses boosted, went to a concert by The Shamen and on to a nightclub afterwards. On another occasion, a friend and I spent the night of Beltane at a sacred site where we had made a small camp-fire and under the influence of Calamus both of us clearly saw little perfectly-formed dragons in the flames. The glowing embers of a charred stick became a fiery serpent and a bit later on we were treated to an extra special dawn chorus!

The Calamus plant has a very strong but pleasant aroma and an overwhelming taste that is hard to describe. Calamus has a certain sweetness as well as a sour quality and a heat like that of ginger tempered with the spiciness of cinnamon.

Calamus can be obtained from many suppliers of herbal products or found growing in the wild, although care should be taken not to confuse it with the similar looking leaves of the Yellow Flag Iris and other reeds and sedges.

The flags, including Sweet Flag, are lunar herbs, ruled by the Moon.

California Poppy
Papaveraceae
Eschscholzia californica

The California Poppy comes from California, as would be expected from its name, but is also found in Mexico and the Southern United States, as well as being cultivated all over the world as an attractive and very easily-grown annual. In fact, so easy is it to grow that it often self-seeds. California Poppy bears beautiful, fairly large and showy flowers

in shades of orange, yellow and red. The leaves are attractive too being blue-green and ferny in appearance.

The flowers of California Poppy contain the mild narcotic alkaloids protopine and altocryptine and when smoked the herb is found to produce a marijuana-like "high." In its home state, some of the Native American tribes have used the California Poppy to ease the discomfort of toothache.

Cannabis
Cannabinaceae /Urticaceae
Cannabis sativa, Cannabis indica, Cannabis ruderalis
Other names: Ashes, Bhang, Blow, Boo, Broccoli, Buddha sticks bush, Charge, Charras, Dagga, Dope, Dry high, Funny stuff, Gage, Gallowgrass, Ganeb, Ganga, Giggles-smoke, Gold, Goof butt, Grass, Griefo, Griffo, Guazza, Has, Hash, Hashish, Hawaiian, Hay, Hemp, Herb, Hooch, Indian hay, Indian hemp, J jay jive joint, Juanita Weed, Kaif, Kauii, Kif, Lamb's Bread, Leaf of Delusion, Locoweed, Love Weed, Mach, Marijuana, Mary, Maryjane, Mary Werner, Mauii, Mex, Mexican, Mezz, Mohasky, Mota, Mu, Muggle, Mutah, Pod, Pot, Red, Reefer, Roach, Rope, Sativa, Shit, Sinsemilla, Skinny, Smoke, Smoke snop, Spliff, Splim, Stick, Stinkweed, Straw, Stuff, Sweet Lucy, Tea,

Texas Tea, Thai sticks, Twist, Viper's Weed, Weed, Wacky baccy,
Whacky baccy, Wheat, Yerba

The Cannabis plant grows all over the world, is used by millions of
people and has a multitude of names, some of which are given above.
It has been used by all cultures that have encountered it for a very wide

variety of purposes. There are very many different types of Cannabis and, as time goes by, many more hybrids and "designer dope-plants" are being developed and cultivated by plant-breeders in an effort to improve potency and yield. The active substance in hemp is known as THC, which is an abbreviated form of delta-9-tetrahydrocannabinol. Sometimes the herb gets mixed with other stronger psychoactive substances like opium and Datura to give it more of a "kick". The countless "stoners", who are always willing to try and buy something new with a bit more kick to it form a ready marketplace.

The *ruderalis* species of Cannabis comes from Siberia and is a short plant, rarely grown. *Cannabis indica* is a bushy variety. It is frequently cultivated and has stronger herbal effects than its cousins. *Cannabis sativa* is the tallest and can grow to as much as 18 foot, although 6 to 10 is more common. This form is mainly cultivated for its fibres to make rope as well as good quality paper and clothing even. Just like with a crop like the grape, there is more than one strain. For example: one type of grape produces currants and another is the white seedless variety, dried as sultanas. So it is with *Cannabis sativa* for one type, commonly referred to as hemp, is cultivated for its fibres for use in rope and cloth-making, while other strains are used for their drug content and are known as marijuana. It is quite important to stress that the hemp type has a very low percentage of THC, as little as 1%, while the marijuana varieties have far more of this active substance, as much as 5%, with many batches of "street" marijuana having upwards of 7% THC content. The plant cultivated by farmers is called "industrial hemp" and because of its very low THC content is very different to the more potent forms grown as marijuana.

The oil is also harvested and, in fact, every part of the Cannabis plant gets used for something. In herbalism it has proved effective for treating depression, anxiety and insomnia and its health-giving properties extend to providing relief from neuralgia, migraine and asthma. Besides these uses Cannabis is also claimed to act as an aphrodisiac.

Cannabis has been successfully employed to treat cases of glaucoma and MS and due to this has sparked further controversy and coverage in the media with regard to sufferers of these complaints using the herb medicinally in countries like the UK where it is illegal. Back in 1976 in

Washington, D.C., Robert Randall, then aged twenty-eight and a part-time teacher, became the first American to win the right to be "exempted from Federal drug laws in order to use marijuana as medicine." Daniel St. Albin Greene in The National Observer covered his story for the week ending July 24th. At a later date a problem arose when he was visiting Britain where this ruling did not apply.

Against a background of a long-fought and on-going public campaign to legalise the herb and its resin, Howard Marks from South Wales, has become something of a celebrity, as well as a figurehead for the cause. He has appeared on countless TV and radio programmes and been much featured in the press, even though, and probably because, he served time in prison for drug offences and is notorious as a man who got rich as a "dope-smuggler". Howard has openly defied the law in the UK and is a household name for his out-spoken stance on the subject. He is also a best-selling author with his autobiography, Mr Nice, lending its name to a new hybrid dope-plant. Nowadays, Howard Marks is making a name for himself as a DJ as well. The Welsh rock-band, The Super Furry Animals, gained a lot of publicity by posing for press-stories with Howard Marks, having pictures of him on one of their hit records, and even dedicating a tribute song to him. The band have another song entitled Northern Lights, which is the name of a well-known type of hybrid "super-dope", as well as that of a spectacular atmospheric phenomenon.

There is a vast amount of literature published about Cannabis and much art, writing and music could be said to have been inspired by this herb. Indeed, many of its common names and slang terminology related to it are almost household words in many places, so widely has its impact on society been felt. In fact, there is a whole jargon of terms used to describe the Cannabis plant and the ways it is commonly employed. For example, "reefer cigarette", used to be the name for a ready-rolled method of smoking it but today "joint" would be a more widespread term for the same thing. "Stoned" means to be under its influence and most people today would understand this slang termi-nology.

Its legal status varies from one country to another and some systems are far more tolerant of Cannabis-users than others. Cannabis use is widespread all over the world despite the efforts of the legal systems to control it, although it is still worth bearing in mind that in many places offences relating to Cannabis can carry a custodial sentence.

Cannabis has a long and colourful recorded history and in the 11th and 13th century AD was employed by a Persian sect of assassins, who while under the influence of the drug, carried out the murder of their victims. Hence, the word "hashish" is linked with the word "assassin" and the Arabic "hasshashin" or "hash-eaters". The herb is recorded in the writings of Pliny and Herodotus, the latter of whom wrote that the Scythians used to roast the seeds and take much pleasure in inhaling the resulting vapours. As far back as 2737 AD, a Chinese ruling-emperor was encouraging his people to use it for medicinal purposes.

Cannabis has even found its way into a religion. Rastafarianism holds the plant in very high esteem as a sacred herb. This religion is also a political movement and started life in Jamaica and the Caribbean. From here it was exported to the world by the reggae music of acts like the late Bob Marley and his band The Wailers. It is a cult centred on Ras Tafari, who is better known as Emperor Haile Selassie of Ethiopia (1930-1947). The belief is that all West Indian Rastafarians came from Ethiopia and that their liberation means returning to the homeland. It is clearly linked with the Biblical story of the Exodus of the Children of Israel from Egypt, the nation that was holding them in bondage. "Dread-locked" followers of the Rastafarian creed smoke large amounts of the herb as a sacred sacrament and to get them closer to Jah. The name for God in Rastafarianism is a variation of the Old Testament patriarchal supreme deity, known as Jehovah or Yahweh. Much of the religion's imagery is taken from Biblical sources and one of the Rastafarian names for Cannabis is "Lamb's bread".

The Cannabis plant is believed to have originated in central Asia and to have spread from there to colonise all parts of the globe. Marijuana is probably the most widely used, and usually illegal, drug that exists. It may well have been native to the northern part of Afghanistan and the Altai mountains of southern Siberia but as it has travelled the world it has changed and adapted to the many different environments it has found. Cannabis plants from America, Asia and Africa can all look very different in appearance. Some of the newly cultivated hybrids are much shorter and more compact than the taller more natural parent plants. Strains from various parts of the world are often given names, which denote their place of origin, such as Acapulco Gold, Durban Poison, Afghani Black, Gainsville Green and Panama Red. Often, the name refers to the processed drug in herbal or resinous form and some types are thought much more highly of than others. A lot of competitive business is fought in the supply of Cannabis and trademarks and patents are common on new varieties for cultivation. There are, rather predictably, shops and mail-order companies that specialise in dealing in these types as seeds and in selling equipment used in cultivation. The seeds are generally legal so these businesses are allowed to carry on. Hemp seed is a staple part of cage and wild birdseed mixes and this often means that seedlings establish themselves in the gardens of people completely ignorant and innocent regarding the matter.

Cannabis grows separately as male and female plants and sometimes it also is found as a hermaphrodite with both male and female branches. Hermaphrodites and male plants usually grow in more adverse circumstances. In the hermaphrodite there is the possibility for self-fertilisation. The pollen of the male-plant is air-born so it could be advantageous for a plant growing in a bad habitat to have male generative organs and to scatter its reproductive efforts to the winds rather than let them fall on barren ground. The Cannabis plant has no need of insects to aid the passing on of its pollen but relies on the air-currents to broadcast its genetic material.

The unfertilised flowering tops of the female Cannabis plant contain the strongest resin and the plant is harvested both as a resin and as herbal "bush", which is allowed to dry out. One interesting aspect of cultivation emerged from the Asian growers, who discovered that if the plant is traumatised when flowering, it reacts by sending larger quantities of the much sought-after resin up into the leaves and topmost parts of the plant. This knowledge has caused the practice of deliberately damaging the growing herb. Twisting the base of the stem so that it breaks causing slits to appear in it does damage to the plant. The stem can also be cut open so a small stone or other object can be inserted and left there. In the Himalayas this "cruel" procedure has been taken even further, where the Cannabis farmer makes "torture baskets" for the upper parts of the young plants. These baskets constrict the plant and its leaves in a tight weave for the rest of its life and from which there is no escape save for its eventual harvest and demise. Whatever may be thought of such a practice it certainly yields a much higher resin production in the treated crop.

The resin is far more potent as an intoxicant and hallucinogen and the oil is stronger still, although the effects of Cannabis vary greatly from one individual to another. Generally speaking, it can be said to be a mild hallucinogen, a relaxant and an appetite stimulant. Many people get the urge to eat a lot after indulging in it and this is known as having an attack of "the munchies".

Many different methods of smoking the herb have been found ranging from hand-held chillums to elaborate water-pipes and hookahs. For those wishing to avoid the potential adverse effects resulting from smoke inhalation, the herb can be taken as a tea or added to cookery recipes such as "hash-cake" and "brownies". It is wise to remember that when consumed internally the potency of Cannabis is considerably increased and can easily result in quite a strong "trip" experience.

The planet Saturn rules the Cannabis plant and it is associated with the deities Bacchus, Pan, Priapus and Vesta.

Catnip
Labiatae
Nepeta cataria
Other names: Cat-mint, Catnep, Catrup, Cat's Delight, Cat's Wort, Field Balm, Nip

This commonly grown member of the Mint and Sage family is often to be found in parks and gardens as well as locally on roadsides, hedge banks and in waste places throughout the UK. It is a perennial plant and flowers in the summer.

Cats love to roll in it and it is one of the plants that have a psychoactive effect on these animals. An old belief holds that Catnip makes cats "frolicsome, amorous and full of battle". It is reported to have a similar effect on us humans too and is usually smoked in a joint or in a pipe or made into a tea. Catnip produces a mild marijuana-like

high but can also be used as a remedy for colds and fevers, flatulence and digestive disorders, anaemia, amenorrhoea and other women's complaints. An old saying states that "if the root be chewed it will make the most quiet person fierce and quarrelsome", so maybe it is best left as a diversion for the cats!

The active constituents in this herb are nepetalic acid, valeric acid, buteric acid, carvacrol, thymol, terpene, dipentene, limonene, lifronella, citral, mepetalacton, metabilacetone, tannins and essential oils.

Catnip is a herb of Venus.

Cinquefoil
Rosaceae
Potentilla reptans

Other names: Crampweed, Creeping Cinquefoil, Fivefinger, Five Fingers, Five finger blossom, Five-leaf-grass, Goosegrass, Goose Tansy, Moor Grass, Pentaphyllon, Sunkfield, Synkefoyle

The Cinquefoil is a very common creeping plant of fields, waysides and other grassy areas. It is found all over Europe, the Mediterranean, Siberia, Asia and North America. Like the name suggests it bears its

leaves in rather attractive groups of five. Cinquefoil produces yellow flowers in May and continuing throughout the summer months.

Although the herb has no narcotic or psychoactive properties the Cinquefoil is included here because it has played a large part in witch-craft being added to flying ointments and an ingredient for spells and magic potions. This is probably because of the mystical associations of the number five although possibly it may have specific shamanic qualities when combined with other herbal ingredients. One such recipe for a flying ointment called for proportions of Cinquefoil, Aconite, Belladonna, Hemlock, Parsley (*Carum petroselinum*) and Cowbane (*Circuta virosa*). With powerful and dangerous herbs like some of these, whatever effect it was supposed to have would be very minor unless it was for some specific magical property that it was included.

Cinquefoil has many uses in folk magic. It is believed that if a seven-leafed specimen of Cinquefoil is found and placed under a pillow, a person sleeping on this will dream of their future lover. A bag of the dried herb hung by a bed is credited with ensuring a good night's rest. Placed above a doorway or sprinkled around a property it can provide protection for all those living within. Carrying the herb is believed to bestow the gifts of luck with love, prosperity, health, power and wisdom. An infusion of the herb used to bathe the head and hands nine times will supposedly break any curses or hexes placed upon the user. Carried into a court of law by a defendant it ensures that the court officials will look favourably upon the bearer's case. Cinquefoil was once employed as an ingredient for a special fishing-bait. Corn was boiled in water with Marjoram (*Origanum vulgare*) and Thyme (*Thymus vulgaris*) and then Nettles (*Urtica dioica*), Cinquefoil and the juice of a Houseleek (*Sempervivum tectorum*) were added. It was believed that no fish could resist this bait and a heavy catch was thus, supposedly, ensured. If any of that is true then it certainly is a most powerful magical herb and definitely deserves to be included here!

The Cinquefoil has medicinal properties too. It is an astringent and is employed as a treatment for skin complaints and also for diarrhoea. The whole herb and root can be used for treating fevers and influenza. An infusion of Cinquefoil root, with its astringent properties, makes a good mouthwash.

Cinquefoil is associated by pagans with the Mother Goddess, and is ruled by the planet Jupiter.

Columbine
Ranunculaceae
Aquilegia vulgaris
Other names: Culverwort, Granny's Bonnets, Lion's Herb

This plant is only included here because it is known in Chinese medicine to possess narcotic properties, probably due to the hydro-cyanic glycosides in it. Columbine is generally regarded as poisonous and is no longer recommended for internal ingestion. It has been used to treat jaundice and diseases of the liver and gall bladder as well as chronic skin complaints and menopausal ailments. Columbine is used in homeopathy against hysteria and nervous disorders.

It is a most decorative perennial plant often grown in gardens in many of its colourful cultivated forms. Columbine can be found growing wild in moist meadows, woods and scrub land in some places. It grows throughout Europe, parts of Asia and in America.

Columbine's scientific name *Aquilegia*, derives from the Latin for eagle but it is also associated with the dove (Columba) of its common

name, and it is, therefore, a herb considered to embody both the fierceness of the eagle and the gentleness of the dove, or the qualities of love and courage.

One more herb of Venus, the Goddess of Love.

Common Reed
Graminaceae
Phragmites australis (Ph. communis)

This common and invasive marsh plant growing up to 5 foot, is thought to contain tryptamine in its rhizomes and if this is correct then it could be used as a psychoactive plant. Many other species in the Graminaceae do contain related alkaloids so it bears investigation.

Common Reed is associated magically with the deities, Ra and Pan, and was believed by the Celts to be connected with the underworld. Common Reed is ruled by the Sun.

Corydalis
Fumariaceae/Papaveraceae
Corydalis cava (C. bulbosa)

This perennial plant is another common plant in gardens and in flowerbeds in parks. Corydalis grows wild in Britain only as an escape, although it is to be found all over Europe.

Corydalis is listed here because it contains the alkaloids, bulbo-capnine and corydaline, which can cause hallucinations, however, there

doesn't appear to be much information on these effects recorded with regard to this herb.

Corydalis has been used in medicine to treat Parkinson's disease and other neurological disorders as well as having been an ingredient in anaesthetic preparations. It is considered too toxic for domestic use.

D

Damiana
Turneraceae
Turnera diffusa /Turnera aphrodisiaca
Other names: Mexican Damiana

Damiana is an aromatic shrub native to Texas and Mexico. It is also found growing in other parts of sub-tropical America and Africa. It has pale green ovate leaves with hairy ribs and yellow flowers arising from the leaf axils. The leaves and stems are harvested while the plant is in flower. Damiana has a bitter flavour and tastes similar in some ways to figs. It yields a greenish volatile oil that smells like Chamomile.

The Damiana herb is used as an aphrodisiac and tonic for the reproductive organs. Mexican women take it as a tea an hour before having

sexual intercourse. It is known to strengthen the nervous system too and is useful for treating depression and anxiety. Damiana definitely needs to be used in moderation, though, because too much of it taken internally can damage the liver.

Many people find that Damiana produces a mild marijuana-like high when smoked or taken as a tea and it has a reputation as a cheap legal alternative to Cannabis. For a tea about two tablespoons of the dried herb are steeped in a pint of water. As a smoke it may be found to be somewhat harsh and a water-pipe may be beneficial.

Damiana is a popular herb and readily available from health-stores and herbal suppliers.

Pluto rules Damiana and its associated deities are Artemis, Diana, Ganesha, Vishnu and Zeus.

Deadly Nightshade
Solanaceae
Atropa Belladonna

Other names: Banewort, Belladonna, Black, Black Cherry, Cherry, Daft-berries, Devil's Cherries, Deadly Dwale, Death's Herb, Devil's Berries, Devil's Herb, Divale, Dwale, Dwaleberry, Dway Berry, Fair

Lady, Great Morel, Manicon, Mekilwort, Murderer's Berry, Naughty Man's Cherries, Sleeping Nightshade, Sleepy Nightshade, Sorcerer's Berry, Sorceror's Cherry, Witches Berry

The Deadly Nightshade is probably the most well known poisonous plant in the UK, even though it isn't that easy to find. This is perhaps a good thing for its bad reputation is based on a grim reality, containing as it does, several very toxic substances and offering us the temptation of its shiny black berries looking a bit like cherries. The berries are also very sweet to the taste and therefore pose a particular threat to children. Deadly Nightshade is often confused with the less toxic, but still dangerous Bittersweet or Woody Nightshade (*Solanum dulcamara*).

Deadly Nightshade is a perennial shrubby herb of woods, thickets and hedges, growing mainly on chalky soils and can also be found throughout Europe and in Asia and North America.

Legends tell that the Devil himself tends the plant in his spare time, with the only night that he can be diverted from this being Walpurgis, when he is too busy getting ready for the witches Sabbath.

The scientific name of Deadly Nightshade – *Atropa belladonna* - derives from Atropos, one of the Fates in Greek mythology, who held the shears to cut the thread of human life. There is a tradition, which states that ancient British priests drunk an infusion before worshipping and invoking Bellona, the goddess of war, and so the second part of the name might be a corruption of this.

The medicinal use of Deadly Nightshade has been in the treatment of hypotension, asthma, abdominal ulcers and spasms, for hyperacidity and many other disorders. It is contained in several proprietary medicines and also has been widely used as a vital aid to ophthalmic diagnosis and surgery, as it dilates the pupils of the eye. Because of this, Deadly Nightshade has been used in the past by Italian women to add to their charms and this, it is believed, lead to them christening the plant as "bella donna", which translates as "beautiful lady". Deadly Nightshade is used in homeopathy too but here, of course, the dosage is very minute.

Deadly Nightshade contains the tropane alkaloids, atropine, scopolamine and hyoscyamine as well as belladonnine, atropamine and atrosin. These are dangerous poisons with terrible and lethal side effects as well as psychedelic properties.

Scopolamine is used as a "truth drug" to obtain information from disorientated prisoners under interrogation. Atropine is a powerful nerve poison. Overdose potential is very high and causes flushed skin, dry mouth, lack of co-ordination, vomiting, delirium, convulsions, respiratory failure and death. A peculiar symptom of Belladonna poisoning is the complete loss of voice, and survivors of such a poisoning can be left with permanent damage to their sight and brain. The "trip" is hardly worth the risks involved and Deadly Nightshade is a plant that is definitely not recommended for experimental usage.

It is reported that its toxic effects can be considerably diminished if the patient swallows an emetic, like warm vinegar or mustard and water, as soon as possible, to make them vomit. Otherwise in a full-blown poisoning by Deadly Nightshade a stomach pump is resorted to, followed by magnesia and a stimulant such as strong coffee. The recovering person is then to be kept warm and artificial respiration may also be necessary.

Horses, sheep, goats, rabbits and pigs are all pretty much immune to Deadly Nightshade but cats and dogs are poisoned just like humans. Buchanan relates in the History of Scotland (1582) concerning the tradition that when Duncan I was king of Scotland that Macbeth's soldiers poisoned a whole army of invading Danes with the aid of this plant. It was a time of truce and the poison was mixed in liquor served to the enemy troops.

Deadly Nightshade has been used in the "flying ointments" of witches as well as in various potions and spells but it is a magical plant connected strongly with the darker aspects of life and death.

Deadly Nightshade is ruled by Saturn and associated with the deities, Atropos, Bellona, Circe, Dionysus and Hecate.

Dogwood
Cornaceae
Cornus sanguinea, Cornus stolonifera
Other names: Red Willow

The Dogwood is included here because the dried bark of its North American and Canadian cousin the Red Osier Dogwood (*Cornus stolonifera*), is smoked by the Plains Indians, for an effect "similar to opium". A decoction from the bark was also used as a stimulant by the North Carrier Indian tribes. These North American Indians call Dogwood "Kinnikinnick", although this term is also used for the ingredients of other "herbal Tobacco", including the Bearberry, as already detailed in this work. Other parts of herbs used in these smoking mixtures are the flowers of Pearly Everlasting (*Anaphalis margaritacea*), and the Wooly Yarrow (*Achillea lanulosa*) as well as the leaves of Yew (*Taxus brevifolia*). The potential psychoactive constituents and properties of these additional forms of Kinnikinnick are unclear.

It is possible that the British variety of Dogwood has similar properties although the shrub is chemically obscure, regarding its active constituents.

The Dogwood is a common enough deciduous shrub found growing in woods, plantations, hedgerows and scrub-land throughout Britain and northern Europe as well as America.

Doñana
Cactaceae
Coryphantha macromeris

The Doñana cactus is small and spiny and found growing in southern Texas and northern Mexico. Like several other members of its family it contains psychoactive constituents that have been known about and utilised by various North and Central American Indian tribes for shamanic purposes.

In this particular plant, the active substance is macromerine, which is a phenethylamine very similar in its effects to mescaline (covered later in the section on Peyote). It is, however, about a fifth of the potency per gram of its better-known cousin. In effect, this means that about eight to twelve fresh whole Doñana cacti must be consumed to experience a similar "trip". The spines must first be removed and then the cactus is either chewed and then swallowed, or can be brewed as a tea for about an hour. It is best taken on an empty stomach because nausea and vomiting are likely. However, this reaction will not affect the intensity of the psychedelic experience. The "trip" may well last up to twelve hours and there are no dangerous side effects apart from obvious psychological problems that may occur, depending on the individual makeup of the consumer. Doñana should not be used in very large quantities, however, nor should it be taken at the same time as any known MAO inhibitors, which are detailed in a later section of this work. Besides macromerine, this cactus contains normacromerine, N-formylnormacromerine, tyramine, N-methyl-tyramine, hordenine, N-methyl-3,4-dimethoxy-B-phenethylamine, metanephrine and synephrine a precursor to the main active constituent.

Other species in the Doñana family that contain psychoactive alkaloids, including macromerine, are *C. pectinada*, *C. elephantideus*, *C. runyonii* and *C. cornifera var. echinus*. Most of these alkaloids, apart from macromerine, are to be found in other types of *C. cornifera*, as well as in *C. duragensis*, *C. ottonis*, *C. poselgeriana* and *C. ramillosa*.

Ergot
Clavicipitaceae
Claviceps purpurea

Ergot is a parasitic fungus that infects grains of rye, barley, wheat and other species of grass and it contains the alkaloid ergine (d-lysergic acid amide), which is better known as natural LSD. The more potent synthetic LSD (d-lysergic acid diethylamide), also known as LSD 25, was originally synthesized from natural psychoactive alkaloids found

in Ergot.

Swiss chemist Albert Hofmann, back in 1938, was studying the Ergot fungus and when he added diethylamide he produced lysergic acid diethylamide. Five years later, when repeating synthesis of the substance Hofmann discovered the psychedelic effects of LSD after accidentally absorbing some through his fingertips on April 16, 1943.

Ergot, which is found growing on grasses and cereals worldwide, forms a dark purplish-brown fungal mass called a sclerotium where the rye or other grain would normally develop. One or more of these pellet-like sclerotia can be seen in an infected grain spike, typically extending out from the rest of the head, and the sclerotia are the source of the potent alkaloids in Ergot.

Thousands of people in Europe in the Middle Ages suffered from an outbreak of Ergotism, a disease characterized by gangrene, convulsions, madness and death. The afflicted people had eaten rye bread infested with Ergot, which also contains other potentially dangerous alkaloids of the Ergotamine group (including Ergotamine, ergosine and ergocristine) that affect blood vessels.

Ergotism became known as "St. Anthony's Fire", and was a dreaded disease in Europe. At one period of history more than 50,000 people died of this disease in France alone. Ergot poisoning can also cause severe hallucinations and insanity.

It has been suggested that "Kykeon", the beverage consumed by participants in the ancient Greek Eleusinian Mysteries, might have included Ergot as a psychoactive ingredient.

Although Ergot is a dangerous poisonous fungus alkaloids in it have been used in medicine to treat uterine bleeding, whilst in homeopathy it is used for circulatory disorders.

F

Fennel
Umbelliferae
Foeniculum vulgare
Other names: Fenkel, Ferny Plant, Finkle, Seaside, Sweet Fennel, Wild
Fennel

Fennel is a most attractive ferny perennial herb that grows wild on
waste ground, along roadsides and almost anywhere by the sea. It has
a strong anise seed flavour and aroma and has long been used for
culinary purposes as well as in perfumes and cosmetics. It is also an
excellent medicinal herb.

The plant is included here because like Dill (*Anethum graveolens*) and
Parsley, two other members of the same family, the seeds and concentrated oil contain myristicin, a drug also found in Nutmeg (*Myristica
fragrans*) and known to have hallucinogenic effects. The amount needed
is such that other decidedly harmful symptoms of poisoning also set in
with convulsions being commonplace. The user also risks severe
damage to the kidneys and liver and the use of these herbs like this
obviously cannot be recommended.

Actually there is an old rhyme, which states: "Fennel, Vervain, Mugwort (*Artemesia vulgaris*) and Dill hinder witches of their will", but the truth of this is open for debate, especially, when it is considered that all these herbs have often been used by practitioners of witchcraft.

Fennel is safe in cooking, however, and is added to curries and vegetable and fish dishes. The herbal tea prepared from it is a very pleasant drink and is good for cases of indigestion and colic, for loss of appetite and for coughs and colds. It is also reported to be of great benefit to the eyesight and as an infusion has been used to soothe eyes inflamed by conjunctivitis. An infusion of Fennel can be used as a gargle or mouthwash as well. There is a tradition that holds Fennel up as a good remedy for obesity. It was once used by the Romans to increase stamina and courage. Fennel is believed to be a herb of protection used to ward off evil spirits and also beneficial as an antidote for snakebites and the poisonings from toadstools.

Fennel contains anethole and fenchone, essential oils, fatty oils, albumin, coumarin derivatives and sugar. Fennel is diuretic and expectorant in its actions and also relieves spasms in the body.

Fennel is a herb ruled by the planet Mercury, and sacred to the deity, Apollo.

Fly Agaric
Agaricineae
Amanita muscaria
Other names: Death's Head, The Woodpecker of Mars

This brightly coloured fungus is familiar to everyone from the illustrations to be found in fairy-story books. Fly Agaric is commonly found in autumn in birch-woods and under pines in thin woodlands and is a most eye-catching mushroom with its large caps of scarlet or deep red, mottled with conspicuous white warts. If any toadstool was to be associated with magic and the fairy kingdom it had to be the Fly Agaric! And rightly so, because this otherworldly looking fungus is perhaps the oldest hallucinogenic plant known, having been in recorded use for over six thousand years. Fly Agaric has been adopted by many cultures, in the Northern hemisphere worldwide, to transport

the partaker into visionary realms.

Fly Agaric has been identified as the soma of ancient India's Vedic culture and religion. R. Gordon Wasson wrote a book, published in 1967, called Soma, Divine Mushroom of Immortality, which examines in depth, the history and effects of this amanita fungus.

Fly Agaric is believed to have been employed as a shamanic aid by the Vikings, and is known to have been, and continuing to be in use, by the tribesmen of Siberia. There is evidence that the ancient Druids and priests of Britain incorporated psychedelic mushrooms into their rituals and this is very likely to have been one of the ones they were aware of.

Fly Agaric contains ibotenic acid and its derivative, muscimol, and also muscazone, hyoscyamine and bufotenine. There has been a lot of debate concerning the toxicity of this mushroom, and as to which of the substances it contains are responsible for the intoxicating and hallucinogenic effects, but one thing seems to have been established, that the Fly Agaric should be dried out thoroughly before consumption. This may well be so that the more poisonous ibotenic acid is transformed into the less toxic muscimol in the drying process.

In a heroic hymn of the Vogul people the "two-belted" hero addresses his wife, saying: "Woman, bring me in my three sun-dried Fly Agarics!"

Most literature on fungi list this species as poisonous and great care needs to be taken with it, even down to the proper identification as there are many other agarics that can be lethal. Also there is no effective antidote to amanita poisoning. This is because amanita toxins take up to twelve hours to take effect and by then it is too late to reverse their deadly course. The Fly Agaric takes its name from the once common practice of using it as an insecticide in the form of fly-paper.

As a matter of interest, atropine (the poisonous hallucinogenic drug already discussed in the section on Deadly Nightshade) has been thought to be a remedy for Fly Agaric poisoning. This is very unlikely as it is known to add to the effects of the toxic ibotenic acid and has also been found to be already present in the mushroom's constituents.

As for bufotenine, although this is a psychoactive substance related in chemical structure to DMT and psilocybin and found in the skins of toads, the amount present is so small in the Fly Agaric as to be insufficient to cause anything noticeable. However, the amphibians' skins have been smoked and brewed for this mind-altering ingredient in many parts of the world. It seems very apt that the substance, bufotenine, is found in toadstools and that both the fungi and the amphibians have connections with witchcraft and magic. There is actually a family of toads with the scientific name of bufo, establishing the link even further.

One to three dried mushrooms appears to be the usual dose and the initial effects should be felt in about twenty minutes with nausea, numbness, confusion, dizziness and a dryness in the mouth occurring. Drowsiness may well set in with an actual period of twilight sleep in which visions may be experienced. After this, vivid visual and auditory distortions, a wavy and alive quality to inanimate objects and a feeling of great mental clarity will be perceived, along with an energised and jovial state of being. The entire experience lasts about eight hours.

Smoking Fly Agaric will produce a milder version of the trip. Obviously effects will vary from one person to another and this should always be considered in the use of such powerful plants. The fresh agaric is thought to be much more poisonous and even in small amounts will produce actual sickness.

It was the practice of Siberian and other tribes to recycle the urine of someone who had already ingested the fungus, and thus, because a substantial amount of the active substances in it remain unchanged, it could be used again or saved for later.

The Fly Agaric is related to and similar in appearance to the Panther Cap (*A. pantherina*) but this latter species is more of a brown colour and contains less psychoactive constituents and more in the way of toxins, and is therefore best avoided.

The Fly Agaric makes an appearance in the world of movies in the 1970 film Performance, directed by Nicholas Roeg and Donald Scammell and starring Rolling Stone Mick Jagger as an ex-rock star. James Fox, who plays a gangster, is introduced to Jagger's world of altered reality and decadence under the influence of the brightly coloured hallucinogenic mushroom.

Mercury rules the Fly Agaric and it is in the sign of Leo.

Fumitory
Fumariaceae
Fumaria officinalis, Fumaria Indica
Other names: Beggart, Beggary, Earth Smoke, Fumiterry, Fumus, Fumus Terrae, God's Fingers and Thumbs, Kaphnos, Kapnos, Lady's Lockets, Nidor, Scheiteregi, Taubenkropp, Vapour, Wax Dolls

Fumitory is an annual weed with straggling stems and finely divided silvery grey-green foliage. It is found growing in fields, scrubland, waste-places, hedgerows and on cultivated land in Europe, the Near East, Asia, Africa, Australia and America so has pretty much colonised the globe. This is appropriate considering the belief of the ancients, who called it "Earth Smoke", considering that it arose from the vapours of the Earth and the inner spirit of the planet, rather than being produced from seed. Fumitory is self-fertile and nearly every seed has the power of germination. Because of this it can spread exceedingly rapidly, again like smoke! Fumitory blooms between April and October with spikes of small pinkish flowers. It has a bitter, saline and somewhat unpleasant flavour.

Fumitory is used in herbal medicine to treat stomach problems, liver complaints and skin disorders. It is a tonic, diuretic and with prolonged

use has strong sedative and narcotic properties. The leafy stems and flowers of Fumitory are harvested and dried in bunches and as an infusion it can be used externally to treat eczema and as a lotion for sunburn, as well as helping to clear spots and freckles. Its juice has been said to be useful for clearing the eyes, possibly by bringing tears to them first and thereby washing impurities and offending matter out. The American species *F. indica* has the same properties but is bitterer in flavour and is more potent. Fumitory contains the alkaloid fumarine, which is thought to be identical to corydaline - see section on Corydalis earlier on in this work.

John Hill, M.D. (1756), once stated: "Some smoke the dried leaves in the manner of Tobacco for disorders of the head with success" .

It was once believed that Fumitory, if burned, had the power of expelling evil spirits and therefore the herb has been used for cases of exorcism. Fumitory was burned for these purposes in the famous geometrical gardens of St.Gall. In relation to this belief about it, the plant has also been employed as a herb of consecration and protection. For such purposes it can be added to incense intended for work like this. Fumitory is a herb of Samhain (Halloween) and can be used to aid communication with the other world of spirits at this time.

Fumitory's planetary ruler is Jupiter.

G

Galangal
Zingaberaceae /Scilaminae
Kaempferia galanga /Alpinia officinarum (Hance)
Other names: Catarrh Root, China Root, Colic Root, East India Root,
Galanga, Gargaut, India Root, Lesser Galangal, Maraba

Galangal is a relative of the ginger plant and comes from China (the island of Hainan), India, Africa and Malaysia. It is a stemless herb, which grows to about 5 foot in height with long blades for leaves and curious white flowers with red veins borne on terminal spikes. The rhizomes of Galangal are reddish-brown and are the part that is harvested. They are cut while fresh into pieces between one and a half and three inches in length.

Galangal had been used in Europe for seven centuries longer than its botanical origin has been officially recognised, and it was only in 1870 that specimens from the extreme south of China were examined and identified as this medicinal and culinary herb. In herbal medicine it has been used to treat flatulence and digestive disorders as well as a stimulant. Galangal has been recommended as a remedy for seasickness

and also to stop bouts of vomiting. The rhizome is pungent and spicy and similar to its relative the ginger-root. In fact, Galangal has often been used as flavouring in ginger beer. Galangal contains a volatile oil, resin, galangol, kaempferid, galangin, alpinin and starch. Powdered it has been taken as snuff in India and it is a favourite spice and medicine in Lithuania and Estonia. In Russia the Tartars brewed Galangal as a tea.

Galangal's name comes from the Arabic "khalanjan", which is perhaps a corruption of the Chinese word for "mild ginger". The Arabs used it to make their horses fiery in spirit and it has been employed in cattle medicine as well as for treating humans.

Galangal has been used as a vision-producing herb by the shamans of New Guinea and in occult practice it has been employed to contact spirit guides and allies. Galangal is a mild hallucinogen but the psychoactive constituents of the herb are not known. The whole rhizome can be chewed and the juice then swallowed or it can be made into an infusion. One tablespoon of the rhizome is used per half-pint of boiling water. Galangal has also found favour as incense for increasing physical and magical energy.

Galangal is a herb governed by the planet Mars.

H

Hawkweed
Compositae
Hieracium pilosella
Other names: Haret Hogeurt, Mouse-ear Hawkweed, Mouse-ear,
Pilosella

The Mouse-ear Hawkweed is a common and widely distributed flower found growing on sunny banks, on walls, at roadsides and in dry pastures throughout northern Europe. It is an annual and blooms from May to September with yellow flowers like Dandelions, carried on stems arising from the base rosette of leaves. Hawkweed is bitter and acrid to the taste.

Mouse-ear Hawkweed has been used in herbal medicine for

enteritis, influenza, pyelitis and cystitis but is rarely prescribed nowadays. It contains a glycosidal bitter principle (umbeliferone), tannin, mucilage and resin, and is a mild diuretic, an astringent and is anti-inflammatory in its action. In North America Mouse-ear Hawkweed has been used by the Iroquois tribe as an anti-diarrhoeal herbal remedy.

According to a Danish text it is psychoactive with around one gram of dried leaves smoked producing an "expanded consciousness without hallucinations".

The herbalist Gerard, writes in his General History of Plants, that a decoction of the herb is so useful that "if steel-edged tools red hot be drenched and cooled therein, oftentimes it makes them so hard that they will cut stone or iron be they never so hard without turning the edge or waxing dull".

Mouse-ear-Hawkweed is a herb ruled by Saturn.

Hellebore (Black)
Ranunculaceae
Helleborus niger
Other names: Bear's Foot, Christmas Flower, Christmas Herb, Christmas Rose, Fetter-grass, Fetterwort, Melampode

The Black Hellebore is a perennial low-growing herb with dark green shiny leaves and white or pink flowers on stalks arising directly from

the root and appearing in the depths of winter - hence some of its common names. It is not to be mistaken for the False Hellebore (*Adonis autumnalis*), the American or Green Hellebore (*Veratrum viride*) or the White Hellebore (*Veratrum album*), although all the hellebores share a similarity in one way, for they are all dangerous poisonous plants. The Black Hellebore is native to southern and Eastern Europe but was first introduced into Britain by the Romans it is believed. Because it is an attractive ornamental plant Black Hellebore is often grown in shrub borders and flowerbeds in parks and gardens. The black part of its name refers to the colour of the freshly dug roots. These roots are harvested in autumn. Division of the rootstocks into separate pieces can propagate the plant, although it does not take kindly to being moved and flourishes best if left in the same position. The Black Hellebore prefers a partially shaded and damp situation.

Hellebore has been employed to treat nervous disorders, hysteria and melancholy, although it should be stressed that this herb is very toxic and should never be used except with the guidance of an experienced practitioner of herbal medicine. Black Hellebore contains helleborin and helleborcin, both very dangerous poisons. The former has narcotic properties and a burning acrid taste; the latter has a sweet taste but is a cardiac poison. The herb has drastic purgative and anthelmintic properties but the risk is too great for domestic use.

Hellebore was once known as "Melampode" after Melampus, a physician of around 1,400 BC. He is said to have prescribed the herb for nervous disorders and hysteria. According to a Greek tradition Melampus was originally a herdsman who realised the properties of the Hellebore after observing the effects it had on his herd of goats. He is reported to have used the milk of these goats, after they had been eating the herb, to cure the mental derangement of the daughters of Proetus, King of Argus.

The ancient Greeks were very careful and ceremonial in their harvesting of the Hellebore's roots. They first drew a magic circle around the plant while chanting incantations to their deities before lifting the roots. Legend states that witches were similarly respectful and cautious when collecting Hellebore. The witch harvesting the herb would be dressed in white and barefoot and would never cut the plant, rather it would be plucked from the soil with the right hand and then transferred to the left. Hellebore was often in the recipes for flying ointments and other potions along with other poisonous shamanic herbs. Hellebore was scattered on the floor by sorcerers who wished to make themselves invisible, and it was waved over cattle to protect the beasts from evil influences.

Hellebore is associated with the deities Athene and Hecate and is another shamanic herb ruled by the planet Saturn.

Hemlock
Umbelliferae
Conium maculatum

Other names: Bad Man's Oatmeal, Beaver Poison, Bunk, Cambuck, Conium, Hecklow, Hemleac, Hemlic, Humlock, Hylic, Keckies, Kex, Musquash Root, Poison Hemlock, Poison Parsley, Spotted Corobane, Spotted Hemlock, Water Parsley

Hemlock is a tall biennial herb from the Parsley family that is found growing along roadsides, in waste places, woodlands and damp habitats such as riverbanks. It can grow to as much as seven foot high and has clusters of small white flowers between June and August. A

good way to distinguish the plant is by the foetid mouse-like smell it emits and by the dark purplish spots that pepper the stems. It is also a very tall plant. It is important to be able to know the Hemlock from some of its similar cousins because, like the last herb covered in this book, it is a dangerous poison. Other related plants that bear some resemblance are Chervil (*Anthriscus cerefolium*), Fennel, Parsnip (*Pastinaca sativa*), Caraway (*Carum carvi*) and Carrot (*Daucus carota*) but whereas these herbs are wholesome, and generally speaking to be considered safe, the Hemlock is an entirely different matter. The unpleasant smell and purple spots can be considered as warning signs, meaning that it would be wise to be very wary of this herb. The leaves are long-stalked and feathery at the base, becoming toothed as they grow further up and with shorter stems. The root is long and tapering. Hemlock is found in Britain, Europe, Asia and North Africa and has been introduced into both South and North America.

Medicinally, Hemlock has been used to treat spasmodic ailments like epilepsy, chorea and acute mania. Also it has been a treatment for whooping cough. It contains the poisonous alkaloid coniine together with several others such as conhydrine and methyl-coniine. Hemlock has a sedative and narcotic action, but as already pointed out is a very toxic herb and can easily produce complete paralysis and death. In fact it has been used as a means of execution, assassination and suicide. The generic name "conium" is thought to be derived from the Greek "kona", meaning to whirl about and this describes the state of vertigo someone who had eaten it would experience before they died. In ancient Greece it was a herb of execution, while in Rome, mixed with opium, it was a method of suicide for philosophers who wearied of life. One such great sage who died after drinking the juice of Hemlock was Socrates. Apparently, the herb's poisons paralyse the whole body and even the power of speech is lost. However, the mind stays alert till the bitter end so it sounds a most unpleasant way to die.

It is thought that the Hebrew word translated as "gall" in the Bible could mean Hemlock and the ancient Jews are reported to have employed the herb to deaden the agonies of dying criminals, such as those condemned to death by stoning. Also another Biblical link is the belief that the purple spots on its stems represent the mark of Cain, placed on his brow after he murdered his brother Abel. Culpeper stated that Hemlock stopped "lustful thoughts" but this is probably because it stopped all thoughts! All over the world the plant has been associated with evil, death and the dark side and the Russians called it "the Satanic herb".

However, Hemlock has been used as remedy and antidote for strychnine poisoning, based on the fact that its action is directly antagonistic to the toxic properties of the other poison. In medieval times Hemlock was mixed with Betony (*Betonica officinalis*) and Fennel seed and considered a cure for the bite of a mad dog.

The antidotes for Hemlock poisoning are tannic acid, stimulants like coffee, emetics of zinc, mustard or castor oil, and, if necessary, artificial respiration. However, the best antidote is to stay clear of it!

Hemlock has been included here as a shamanic herb because like the Hellebore it was used as an ingredient of recipes for the witches flying ointments. It has also been used to aid astral travel, perhaps all the way over to the other side and quitting the physical body completely! Hemlock has been employed as a herb of consecration and early grimoires suggest that the magician's athame or ritual dagger should be dipped in the blood of a black cat mixed with Hemlock juice before it is used to cast a magic circle.

Hemlock is another poisonous herb ruled by Saturn. Not surprisingly, it is associated with the Goddess Hecate.

Henbane
Solanaceae
Hyoscyamus niger
Other names: Belene, Black Nightshade, Brodswort, Caniculata, Cassilago, Cassilata, Cat-lye, Chenile, Devil's Eye, Deus Caballinus, Dog-piss, Hebenon, Henbell, Hog's Bean, Hog-bean, Hyoscyamus, Isana, Jupiter's Bean, Jusquiasmus, Loaves of Bread, Poison Tobacco, Stinking Roger, Symphonica, Tooth-wort

The Henbane is a very poisonous and dangerous biennial or annual herb. It is sticky and hairy and emits an offensive smell and is found growing locally in waste places, roadsides, railway banks and sand

dunes. It usually grows to about two foot in height but may be shorter and in July it produces curiously attractive pale-yellow flowers veined with purple.

Henbane was one of the ingredients in many of the witches brews and ointments in the Middle Ages. It was also used as a certain poison of execution. Henbane paste is reported to have been smeared on the tips of Celtic arrows. The herb was known to the ancient Greeks, the Romans and the Egyptians and presumably figured in their dark mysteries. The medieval witches thought that it could easily cause permanent insanity and this seems highly likely and something not worth finding out!

The herb Henbane contains the tropane alkaloids, hyoscyamine, scopolamine and atropine, covered in detail elsewhere, and its medical use is the same as for the other plants that contain these potentially lethal compounds.

Henbane has, in the past, been used as a substitute for opium, where the latter drug-plant was thought inappropriate such as in children's complaints. The herbalist Joseph Miller wrote of the Henbane: "The roots are frequently hung about children's necks...to prevent fits and cause an easy breeding of the teeth". Whilst Gerard states: "To wash the feet in a decoction of Henbane causeth sleep, or given in a clyster it doth the same, and also the often smelling to the flowers". He also wrote that "The Seed is used by mountebank tooth-drawers which run about the country, to cause worms to come forth of the teeth by burning it in a chafing dish of coles, the party holding his mouth over the fume thereof; but some crafty companions to gain money convey small lute-strings into the water persuading the patient that these small creepers came out of his mouth or other part which he intended to ease".

The scientific name translates as "the bean of the hog" and apparently these beasts can eat the plant being immune to its poisonous effects. Humans, however, are not hogs and do best by avoiding this herb.

Henbane is ruled by the planet Saturn and is associated in witchcraft with crone aspects of the Goddess. It was Culpeper who placed the herb under the dominion of Saturn because he thought that it grows in Saturnine places: "Whole cartloads of it may be found near the places where they empty the common Jakes and scarce a ditch is found without the growing of it".

Hops
Cannabinaceae/Urticaceae /Morabaceae
Humulus lupulus
Other names: Beer Flower

Hops are well known as one of the main ingredients in ales and beer but they also have a place in herbalism and folk-medicine as well. This climbing perennial plant is common in hedges, thickets, on fences and anywhere it can ramble. It is also cultivated on a vast scale for the brewery industry. It grows as separate male and female plants.

It is one of only two plants in the genus Cannabinaceae with the other being, as the generic name suggests, the Cannabis plant. Indeed, the Hop can be grafted successfully on to a rootstock of Cannabis

producing a plant that looks like a Hop but contains THC, the illegal active ingredient in marijuana.

If smoked in a joint the hop fruiting parts will produce a mild, grass-like high and the whole plant if made into a tea can be used as a tranquilliser or sedative. The dried Hops can also be stuffed into a pillowcase to aid anyone suffering from insomnia. The young leaves and shoots of Hops can be cooked as greens as well.

The active constituents of Hops are lupulin, humulene, lupulinic acid, essential oil and tannins.

Hops should not be taken in excess, however, as too much can have unpleasant side effects such as dizziness and jaundice symptoms. The plant can also exert an anti-aphrodisiac effect, so would-be-lovers take note!

The herb's generic name, "*Humulus*" refers to the fact that it likes a deep soil or "humus" to root in and the "*lupulus*" part signifies "wolf", which is probably because the plant can kill other plants by strangling just like its animal counterpart is a killer too.

The Hop is ruled by the planet Mars and associated with the deities of Brighid and Leto.

J

Japanese Belladonna
Solanaceae
Scopolia japonica

The Japanese Belladonna (*Scopolia japonica*), as its name suggests, from its flowers and the substances it contains, bears a similarity to the Deadly Nightshade, and is actually in the same family of plants. Like its distant cousin it contains various tropane alkaloids including scopolamine, which is also present in Henbane and Thorn Apple, covered elsewhere in this book. These substances give the plant, and its close relatives, narcotic and hallucinogenic properties, but like the Deadly Nightshade they are potentially very dangerous so should not be used for entheogenic purposes.

Scopolia is a genus of five species of similar herbs - *S. carniolica*, *S. japonica*, *S. lutescens*, *S. parviflora* and *S. tangutica* – which are native to Europe and Asia and the genus is named after Giovanni Scopoli (1723-88), who was an Italian naturalist.

European Scopolia, or Russian Belladonna (*Scopolia carniolica*) is a creeping perennial plant, with light green leaves and pale yellow to

dull red flowers that comes from Bavaria, Austro-Hungary, and south-western Russia and is cultivated as garden flower. It grows from a rhizome, and, like Japanese Belladonna, may be distinguished from the true Belladonna, which is a root.

Mrs M. Grieve tells us in A Modern Herbal that "Scopolia is but little used in Britain, but has been used in America for many years in the manufacture of Belladonna plasters".

<h2 style="text-align:center">Juniper</h2>
<h3 style="text-align:center">Cupressaceae</h3>
<h3 style="text-align:center">Juniperus communis</h3>

Other names: Enebro, Genevrier, Gemeiner Wacholder, Ginepro, Horse Saver, Melmot Berry, Mountain Yew

The Juniper is a large shrub or small tree that grows in woods, on moors, hillsides and other wild places with poor or chalky soil throughout Europe, Russia and Scandinavia and in parts of Asia, as well as Canada and North America. It has reddish-brown bark and needles for leaves showing it to be a conifer. It is also frequently culti-vated in parks and gardens and there are many varieties of the Juniper. It can grow to about 18 foot, but is usually smaller and has both male

and female cones on separate trees. In parts of Norway and Sweden the Juniper sometimes attains a height of 36 foot. The female cones develop slowly into blue-black berries, which are the main part of the tree used in herbalism and also in cooking for a distinctive turpentine-like flavouring. These berries can take as much as three years to fully ripen. Besides being the main flavouring for gin it is also used to brew a Swedish beer with health-giving properties.

The ancient Egyptians are said to have employed Juniper as one of the ingredients for their embalming process as well as using it for various medicinal reasons. It has been used as an incense to repel evil and get rid of disease and in Europe the tree is associated with healing and purification.

Juniper is said to act as a mild hallucinogen when smoked and it contains the following substances: alpha pinene, cadinene, camphene, terpenene, sabinal, tannins, resin, flavone and volatile and essential oils.

In herbal medicine it has been found to be a remedy for rheumatic conditions and also for bladder and kidney complaints but the herb should be avoided in pregnancy. It is a strong diuretic, an antiseptic and stimulates digestion. In magic, Juniper has been used in incense as a herb of purification and to banish negative energies. It is associated with truth and justice.

Juniper is ruled by Mars and the Sun and associated with Pan and the Greek avenging Furies.

L

Labrador Tea
Ericaceae
Ledum latifolium, Ledum palustre, Ledum hypoleucum, Ledum groenlandicum

Other names: James's Tea, Marsh Cistus, Marsh Tea, Porsch, St. James's Tea, Sumpfporsch, Wild Rosmarin, Wild Rosemary

Labrador Tea is an evergreen shrub from the heather family that reaches a height of four to five feet and bearing woolly branches. It has smooth dark-green leaves with hairy undersides and rolled-back margins. The large white flowers are produced in terminal clusters in June and July. It grows in bogs, moors and woods in mountainous areas in Greenland, Labrador, Nova Scotia and the Hudson's Bay area of Canada. It is also found in parts of Scotland, North America and in Siberia. The species *latifolium* is taller and has larger leaves than its cousin *L. palustre*.

The latter of these two species has been reported as having been used in the berserker frenzies of the Viking tribes, and the Tungus people of Siberia are said to have preferred this shamanic herb and its effects to the Fly Agaric, which many of their neighbours consumed so

avidly. The dried leaves were burned on a fire or on a pan and the smoke was inhaled in healing sessions and for tribal rituals. The Gilyaks, also from Siberia, are reported to have used the herb in a similar fashion. Over in British Columbia the Kwaikutl Indians employed the species *groenlandicum* for its inebriating properties. In Germany the leaves were used in the brewing process because their narcotic properties gave the beer an extra "kick". During the War of Independence, Labrador Tea (*L. latifolium*) leaves were a regular substitute for ordinary China tea.

In Russia the leaves have been incorporated in the process of tanning leather, while in Lapland the branches are placed in grain stores to keep away mice and rats. Strewed among clothes the leaves and twigs will help prevent attacks by moths.

The herb contains tannins and gallic acid and has been used in herbal medicine to treat coughs and bronchitis as well as for dyspepsia. Externally, as a strong decoction, it has proved effective in cases of itching and skin disease as well as being used to kill lice. Labrador Tea has tonic properties and is an expectorant and diuretic herb.

Lime (Large-leaved)
Tiliaceae
Tilia platyphyllos
Other names: Linden Flowers, Linn Flowers, Flores Tiliae, Tillieul

The Lime Tree is commonly found in parks, woodlands and along roads where it can grow to as much as 130 foot. It has broad leaves and these are often covered in the sticky honeydew of aphids in the late summer months. It flowers from June to July and strongly perfumes the surrounding air with its scent, a scent much loved by bees that collect and convert the lime tree nectar into a marvellous honey.

Its close relatives, the Small-leaved Lime (*T. cordata*) and the Common Lime (*T. europaea*) are similar in appearance and have the same properties.

The part that is harvested and used is the whole flower-head including the "wing". These are dried and used to make teas and infusions and are good for colds and flu (especially when sweating is

desired), as a laxative and to treat nervous complaints and insomnia. The Lime has sedative properties and is excellent as a relaxant. The tea is very popular in France, where it is called "tillieul". Old flowers that have been stored too long may cause a narcotic intoxication.

At one time it was believed that Lime flowers were a cure for epilepsy or "falling-sickness", as it was known. It may well benefit sufferers, however, by reason of its calming properties, so this belief may well have been based on a reality. The herbalists of old were very optimistic though, as they believed that merely sitting in the shade of such a tree could cure an epileptic.

Jupiter rules the Lime tree.

Lobelia
Campanulaceae
Lobelia inflata
Other names: Asthma Weed, Bladderpod, Eyebright, Gagroot, Indian Tobacco, Pukeweed, Rapuntium inflatum, Vomitwort

The Blue-flowered Lobelia is a hardy annual herb from North America, some parts of Canada and also grows in gardens in Europe. *L. dortmanna* is similar and found growing wild in Britain. The Lobelia is

found in dry areas and waste places. The herb is named after Matthias de Lobel, a renowned botanist from Lille, who died in London in 1616.

Lobelia has been extensively used in herbal medicine by the Native American tribes for hundreds of years, as well as in rituals and for shamanic purposes. The Crow employ it in their ceremonies and the Pawnee and Mesquakie use it for love magic. The Penobscot Indians, from New England, made much use of the herb long before Samuel Thomson, who has often been credited as the plant's first discoverer, had found it.

The whole Lobelia herb contains the piperidine alkaloid lobeline as well as lobelamidine and nor-lobelamidine and has expectorant, emetic, anti-asthmatic and stimulant properties. In bronchial and pulmonary disorders it has proved invaluable as, taken as an infusion, it speedily removes any accumulated mucus. An infusion of one ounce of powdered dried herb in one pint of boiling water can be taken in doses of half to a wine-glassful at a time.

Lobelia has been used successfully to treat withdrawals from nicotine and is often a constituent of anti-smoking lozenges. Rather surprisingly, in view of this, it can be smoked for a mild legal marijuana-like high, although the smoke is rather acrid to the taste. Brewed as tea it has stronger effects but may cause nausea and vomiting as well as an unpleasant prickly sensation in the mouth and tingly feelings in the body. It should be taken on an empty stomach and it is well to remember that too much can cause circulation problems, unpleasant side effects and be toxic.

M

Magic Mushrooms
Strophariaceae
Psilocybe lanceolata
Other names: Hombrecitos ("little men"), Liberty Caps, Los Ninos ("the children"), Las Mujercitos ("the little women"), Mushrooms, Noble Princess of the Waters, Psilocybin Mushrooms, Shrooms, She-To

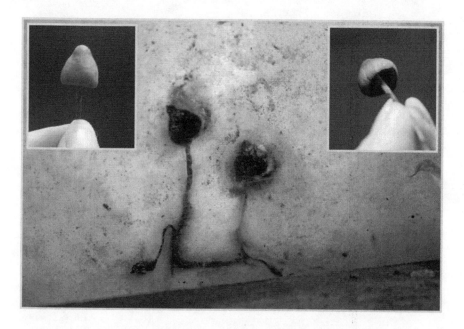

Every autumn, since the late '70s when Magic Mushrooms suddenly became known in a big way amongst recreational drug-users, we've seen warnings in the press about the dangers of these fungi and the authorities in the UK have made possession of the mushrooms, including fresh ones, a Class A drug offence. We've even had "magic mushroom festivals" and a psychedelic rock group called The Magic

Mushroom Band. So nowadays the British psilocybin mushroom or Liberty Cap is a very well known little fungus that grows commonly from September onward in many fields, parks and on grassy hillsides throughout the land. The species also grows in northern Europe, Scandinavia and North America.

Psilocybin mushrooms had already been discovered in psychedelic drug circles and by shamanic cultures worldwide before the '70s boom, and indeed, evidence shows that these fungi and related species have been used in rituals, as a sacrament and for divination by many different tribal groups throughout the history of mankind.

The author and psychonaut, Terence McKenna, has suggested that a symbiotic relationship was set up between the mushroom and human beings when we discovered the fungi growing in the dung of the very first herded cattle and sheep. He further suggests that the ingestion of these fungi played a large hand in the evolution of the human race towards its present capabilities. Whatever the case may be, the magic mushroom is certainly a powerful psychoactive plant that has effects similar to LSD and is the drug of choice for many "trippers". McKenna contributed to a hit record with Re-evolution, a track on Boss Drum an album by top UK psychedelic dance band The Shamen and made appearances with the group, giving interviews linking his theories with the rise in popularity of dance music and the "rave-culture". Psychedelics, in particular ecstasy and LSD, are very popular with people who attend "raves" so many, many people were interested in Terence McKenna's views on the subject.

Writing for an article in Magical Blend magazine, and republished in the British Freakbeat, McKenna had the following to say of the magic mushroom and its shamanic properties:

"Psilocybin is the most commonly available and experimentally accessible of these compounds (psychoactive tryptamines). Therefore my plea to scientists, administrators and politicians who may read my words is this: to look again at psilocybin, to not confuse it with other psychedelics, to realise that it is a phenomenon unto itself with an enormous potential for transforming human beings, not simply transforming the people who take it, but transforming society in the way that an art movement or a mathematical understanding, or a scientific breakthrough transforms society. It holds the possibility of transforming the entire species by virtue of the information that comes through it. Psilocybin is a source of Gnosis, and the voice of Gnosis has been silenced in the Western mind for at least a thousand years".

David Icke, the ex-footballer, sports commentator and spokesperson for the Green Party, now turned conspiracy theorist and author, reveals in his highly controversial book The Biggest Secret, that the magic mushroom was used in mystery school initiations by the Brotherhood of the Essenes, back in the time of Jesus. The Essenes lived at Qumran at the northern end of the Dead Sea and Icke tells us that this ancient brotherhood of mystics had a detailed knowledge of hallucinogenic plants. So highly regarded were these sacred fungi that they were gathered with care before sunrise, and the Jewish priests of the time actually had mushroom-shaped caps, which they wore at religious ceremonies and for rituals. Perhaps this is where the idea for domes for mosques and synagogues originated?

The fungus contains the drug psilocybin (4-phosphoryloxy-N, N-dimethyltryptamine), which is relatively unstable and converts to psilocin (4-hydroxy-N, N-dimethyltryptamine) in the body and produces the psychedelic experience. This was the substance that turned on Timothy Leary, the ex-Harvard professor who turned "acid guru", although he had a Mexican variety of the fungus - *Psilocybe mexicana* - for his first trip. The mushroom is eaten fresh, dried, or taken in a tea with about 10 to 50 of the fungi being a dose. The strength of dosage depends, of course, upon the size and freshness of the mushrooms, the individual's tolerance, whether other foods, drugs or drink have already been ingested as well, and also the setting and psychological state of the consumer. The first effects come on within about 45 minutes and the experience intensifies reaching a peak and then subsiding, lasting between 4 and 8 hours on average. The greater the amount taken the stronger the trip and the longer the experience lasts.

Many people feel that it is a lot easier to handle than LSD, and there is the idea that it is a much more organic drug. Some have expressed the notion that the fungus became widely known in the '70s as a gift from Mother Earth to help make us, her children, more aware of our relationship with the eco-system here and the whole cosmos we inhabit.

Nevertheless, the magic mushroom is to be treated with wisdom and caution, as it is a most powerful mind-altering fungus. Care needs to be taken not to confuse it with other similar small fungi that grow in the same habitats as some of these could cause poisoning and sickness. The Liberty Cap is very distinctive with its characteristic nipple on top and once correctly identified with an "experienced picker", a novice should soon get the knack of recognising it. One test is to lightly crush or break the stem at the base and if it turns a bluish colour the chances are you've got a psilocybin mushroom.

Tolerance to psilocybin mushrooms does develop but there is no physical or psychological dependence risk or possibility of addiction. It has been estimated that 50 pounds of the fresh fungus would have to be eaten for a lethal dose, which is an awful lot of mushrooms! It does have a cross-tolerance with LSD, meaning that the use of one will add to the cumulative tolerance of the other hallucinogen.

There are various other British species that contain psilocybin in varying amounts and the most common of these is the Hay-maker's Mushroom, *Panaeolus foenisecii* (Lawnmowers Mushroom), which is found in lawns, fields and pastures from early summer onwards, often in troops. *P. sphinctrinus* has also been said to contain the drug. This fungus is reported to have been used by the Oaxacan Indians from

Mexico. It is much larger than the Liberty Cap and has a brownish or grey cap. It grows in similar locations in autumn but is usually found on dung.

In North America the species, *P. subalteatus* has found favour with mushroom-users. This mushroom is common from spring to fall on compost, dung and manure piles throughout the continent. It also occurs in rings along roads and on lawns. It reaches about 5 inches in height and has cone-shaped caps of light brown, which flatten as they

mature and become a darker colour at the edges.

Another popular species is *Stropharia cubensis*, which also grows in southeastern Asia and Central and equatorial America. It is found mainly throughout Texas, Louisiana, Alabama, Arkansas, Tennessee, Mississippi, Georgia and Florida, where it grows on dung and rich pasture from February onward. It is a large species attaining 6 inches in height with a conical or bell-shaped cap of a whitish, pale brown or reddish gold colour. It lends itself to easy cultivation and can be grown on mushroom compost, agar-agar or rye grain and it can do so well that it is literally squashed against the sides of the container. This is one of the species that got distributed widely by dealers in magic mushroom-growing kits and spores of the various types until new laws in the UK and elsewhere put a stop to this in many countries. Information on such cultivation is available in books like the classic Psilocybin: Magic Mushroom Grower's Guide, by O.T Oss and O.N Oeric and published by And/Or Press. It is a particularly potent variety of magic mushroom with 1 gram of dried fungus producing 2 milligrams of psilocybin.

Two more species that can be found in the United States are *Psilocybe caerulipes* and *Psilocybe caerulescens*. The former of these is found on rotting logs and around stumps of trees, especially birch and maple. It has a smooth parasol-shaped cap of a cinnamon or dingy brown shade and is quite common in areas in New York, Tennessee and North Carolina. It is also found as far north as Michigan and up into Canada.

The latter of these two species likes a more sub-tropical climate and is found in clusters in newly turned soil and sugar cane mulch in the southern states in the summer rainy season. It grows to about 5 inches with very dark, almost black young caps fading to brown as they mature. It is worth noting that the scientific names of both these species denote their blue-staining nature, which is a good indicator of their psilocybin content.

The common North American species *P. baeocystis* is best avoided. This species also contains the alkaloids baeocystin and norbaeocystin and it is believed that these substances may well have contributed to the death of a six-year old boy that perished in 1960 after eating many of these mushrooms.

A foreign species of Psilocybin mushroom appears to be becoming naturalised in the UK, possibly brought in from America. The often wavy-edged brownish caps of *Psilocybe cyanescens* are much larger than any native British species of Psilocybe, and clumps of the fungus can be found growing on the wood-chip mulch of flower and shrub borders even in the heart of cities. Although the species contains psilocybin and is more potent than the native types, other substances in it may give rise to toxic effects it has been reported, although other people favour this species.

Mandrake
Solanaceae
Mandragora officinalis / officinarum, Mandragora autumnalis
Other names: Alraun, Anthropomorphon, Baaras, Brain Thief, Circejium, Circoea, Dollwort, Dragon-doll, Galenmannchen, Gallows, Gallow's-man, Herb of Circe, Hexenmannchen, Ladykins, Mandragen, Mandragor, Mandragora, Mannikin, Raccon Berry, Semihomo, Sorcerer's Root, Witches Mannikin, Wild Lemon, WoMandrake

The Mandrake is a member of the potato family and like its relatives, the Deadly Nightshade, Thorn-Apple and Henbane, it contains dangerous tropane alkaloids. As is the case with these herbs, it has been

used as an ingredient of witches' brews and in "flying ointments". It is a perennial herb growing to about a foot high and is found in stony and uncultivated ground. The Mandrake is native to southeastern Europe, although it is cultivated throughout the continent. It should not be confused with the American Mandrake or May Apple (*Podophyllum peltatum*). Mandrake has a long root, sometimes growing to as much as 3 feet in length. Like the Ginseng root it can be forked and for someone with a good imagination can be thought to resemble the lower half of a human body. In fact, Pythagoras was said to have called it "anthropo-morph", which means "tiny human being". The root of the Mandrake became associated with the idea of the homunculus. Often, the root was carved to make it more like a human body, and so with these features, it is not at all surprising that it became respected as a magical plant. In France it was thought to represent the elf Mandelgloire, who had the power of bringing wealth. Joan of Arc was accused at her trial of having a Mandrake formed into a mannikin and used as an amulet for magical purposes. Because possession of a Mandrake was thought to bring good luck, unscrupulous people sometimes carved the common white bryony roots into human shapes and sold these to unsuspecting customers for large sums of money.

It is thought that there are Mandrakes of both sexes. The female

Mandrake is often identified as the *autumnalis* species, which bears purple flowers. The Dean of Wells, William Turner (c. 1508-68) wrote in a 16th century herbal that the fruit of the female plant was "well smelling" but that the male did "smell pleasantly joyned to a certain grevousness".

The Mandrake has large ovate leaves arising directly from the ground in a rosette. The flowers are formed on short stalks and are whitish or greenish yellow in colour and bell-shaped. The herb blooms in March and April and the flowers are followed by green apple-like fruits that turn a deep golden-yellow as they ripen. These fruits smell a bit like pineapples.

Mandrake contains hyoscyamine, scopolamine, atropine and mandragorine and has been called a narcotic, a hypnotic and a hallucinogenic. It has also gained a reputation as an aphrodisiac and was mentioned in this connection by Theophrastus back in the 4th century. He stated that the root should be scraped and then soaked in vinegar. Firstly, it was to be gathered while facing the west, after having drawn three magic circles around the herb with the aid of a sword. An assistant danced in a circle reciting magical formulae. A 12th century bestiary even claimed that the herb could stimulate the desire for passion in an elephant. It told how a female elephant, which wished to become pregnant, ate some Mandrake and gave it also to a bull-elephant. The male became amorous soon after and her wish was fulfilled. In some ways this story reminds us of the Biblical tale of Adam and Eve and the apple.

Mandrake was believed to be an excellent aid to fertility, as well as an aphrodisiac, and the Arabs called the root "devil's testicles". In the Bible book of Genesis, Rachel barters with Leah for the Mandrake roots her son has. She wanted to use them to become fertile. Barren women, who believe in its power, still carry the root as charm to help them conceive. In folk-magic it is also worn as an amulet to attract love.

In Pliny's time it was given to people as an anaesthetic before surgery and it does have the ability to deaden pain and cause sleep. Pliny agreed with Theophrastus about harvesting the herb, although he said there was no need for the dancer. He stated, with emphasis, that one should not dig the root with the wind blowing in your face. Beliefs and stories like these make up a small part of the vast folklore that has built up around the plant. In fact, over twenty books have been published about this herb and its properties alone.

It was once believed that so like a human was the Mandrake that it would scream in pain when pulled from the ground. The cry of the plant thus tormented would be so blood-curdling that anyone who heard it would go mad. However, if diggers went to get a root on a Friday before sunrise, safety would be assured if they first closed off their ears with cotton sealed with pitch or wax. The diggers should then loosen the soil from the root and tie it to the tail of a dog that they had brought with them. Bread was to be thrown for the dog to eat while the diggers got out of the way. The dog would then die and the diggers could go back and collect the magical and very dangerous root.

The Mandrake root is the main part of the herb that is used, although the whole plant contains the tropane alkaloids responsible for is effects. If taken internally Mandrake can easily cause very unpleasant side effects like dizziness, headache, nausea, diarrhoea, cramps and extreme confusion as well as hallucinations. Too much will cause a deep trance, which can lead on to insanity and death. In ancient Palestine its soporific properties were used to induce a trance state in those being executed by death on the cross. It was known as "morion" and is thought that as Mandrake wine it was used to soak the sponge that was offered to the crucified Jesus. This is another herb to be approached with great care, as is illustrated by some of the folk-tales surrounding it.

The Mandrake is a herb of Mercury.

Mistletoe
Loranthaceae
Viscum album

Other names: All Heal, Birdlime, Birdlime Mistletoe, Devil's Fuge, Donnerbesen, Golden Bough, Herbe de la Croix, Holy Wood, Lignum Crucis, Misseltoe, Mystyldene, Thunderbesem, Witches Broom, Wood of the Cross

The Mistletoe is almost too well known to need describing, being a

regular sight every Yuletide season. This modern use, however, is a follow on from its Pagan past and it is one of the most sacred and holy herbs of the Druids of old, and those of modern times. It is a very unusual plant being a parasite growing on the branches of trees and deriving its nourishment from them. It is an evergreen and can be seen easily in the winter months when the branches are devoid of leaves. Mistletoe is mainly distributed by songbirds like the thrush, which wipe their beaks, on which the seeds in the sticky berry pulp adhere, on to the branches of trees. It grows in Europe, North Africa and parts of Asia and is usually found on Apple but also on Hawthorn, Ash, conifers and various other trees. It is rarely discovered on Oak and for this reason the ancient Druids attached particular importance to it when they found it on this tree. The Oak was their chief tree with its Celtic name of "duir" giving the root of both "druid" and "door".

Mistletoe was held to be particularly sacred and magical because it grows in a place between the sky and the earth. The berries are fully ripened in December and take on a golden tinge to their white colour. It was then, in mid-winter, that the herb was harvested by a druid cutting it down with one stroke and using a golden sickle. The sickle represented the energy of the sun and the substance of the moon and the druid cutting it would stand on one leg with one arm raised and one eye closed so as to symbolise the between worlds association. It was to be caught on a white cloth to prevent it reaching the earth and grounding its vital energies.

Mistletoe is believed to have been the sacred "golden bough" of the Druids and mentioned in Virgil's Aeneid as the plant Aeneas had to remove from a tree in order to fulfil his quest of entering the Underworld or Hades.

The berries being white and sticky represented the semen of the oak tree and thus lead on to its association with matters of sexual love and fertility and to the modern custom of kissing under the Mistletoe. The Latin scientific name actually translates as "sticky white".

After it had been cut down Mistletoe was used as a panacea and cure-all for the people of the tribes. Today it still has medicinal uses as a tonic, a diuretic, narcotic and for relieving spasms and lowering blood pressure. Mistletoe has been found to be very effective in cases of epilepsy or "falling sickness" as it was once known. It is also used in small doses as a herb to relax the nervous system, though it should be taken in moderation under the close supervision of a herbalist or medical practitioner. Too much can have a toxic effect and the berries are particularly poisonous. It contains viscotoxin, arginine, choline, acetylcholine, beta phenylethylamine, tyramine and fatty oil. Several of these substances influence the brain and nervous system, hence its powers as a relaxant.

It was very much an original plant of "love and peace", as at Solstice and the time of the cutting of the Mistletoe, Celtic rules stated that all warfare and strife had to cease. This idea also got incorporated later on into the hanging of Mistletoe at the season of goodwill and the birthday of the Christian Prince of Peace.

It is ruled by the Sun and the planet Jupiter and has associations with the following deities: Apollo, Balder, Cerridwen, Frigga, Freya, Odin and Venus.

Monkshood
Ranunculaceae
Aconitum napellus

Other names: Aconite, Cupid's Car, Chariot of Venus, Dumbledore's Delight, Friar's Cap, Friar's Cowl, Helmet Flower, King's Coach, Old Wife's Hood, Queen Mother of Poisons, Storm Hat, Wolf's Bane

The Monkshood or Aconite is a hardy perennial herb of woods, thickets, riverbanks and shady places, which suit its very sinister nature for this plant is, without a doubt, the most dangerous poisonous plant in this book. Nevertheless, it is quite commonly grown in gardens and parks where it could pose a particular danger. It should really be kept well away from children and pets, as this plant is a potential killer. As a hallucinogen it is simply not worth the risk as the trip you'd get from it could very well be your last one. The plant is so toxic that it is a good idea to wash your hands if you handle it and be very careful indeed in all dealings with this herb. My advice would be to simply appreciate the dark beauty of its purple or blue helmet-shaped flowers and glossy divided leaves. It is good to look at but not a plant to touch without the greatest of care!

Monkshood is a herb that has many associations with witchcraft and is another ingredient in "flying ointment". It has often been used as a poison too. Pope Adrian VI was murdered with this and there was an assassination plot against Alexander the Great using Aconite. In Greek myth Medea is said to have poisoned the cup of Theseus with this deadly herb. Even the Prophet Mohammed is reported to have narrowly escaped death when he gave away a piece of poisoned meat meant for him.

The name "Wolf's Bane" derives from its use as in poisoned bait for these animals and also on the tips of arrows used in hunting.

A story from Christian lore links the plant with St. Dunstan, the archbishop of Canterbury, who is said to have once had a prophetic dream in which a great tree, covered in monk's cowls was seen to stretch right over Britain. He thought this symbolised the future domination of the land by the Christian church.

It has the following constituents: aconine, aconitine, neopelline,

picratonitine, benzoylamine, tannins and resin and is classified as an irritant sedative effecting the central nervous system.

Monkshood is contained in some modern brands of medicine but is used with extreme caution by the medical profession. It also has a place in homeopathic remedies but here again the dose given is very minute and under strict supervision. Monkshood is definitely not to be used for domestic purposes. Poisoning with Monkshood causes a burning sensation on the tongue and in the mouth, stomach pain and vomiting, paralysis and finally death.

Monkshood is a herb of Saturn and associated with the deities of the Underworld, Hecate and Cerberus.

Mormon Tea
Gnetaceae /Ephedraceae
Ephedra viridis, Ephedra sinica, Stapf., Ephedra equisetina, Bunge., Ephedra gerardiana, Wall. (Indian), Ephedra nevadensis
Other names: Ephedrine, Jointfir, Ma Huang, Teamster's Tea

Species of this herb grow in waste places and on shorelines in northern China, India and some of the southern states of North America. Mormon Tea is a brittle-looking, slender plant with a very primitive appearance. The leaves are reduced to sheaths surrounding the jointed stems, which bear about twenty tufts of 6-inch needles. The flowers are very insignificant.

Mormon Tea is possibly the earliest plant used for psychoactive properties in human history and has been discovered as pollen remains in a 50,000-year-old Neanderthal grave in a Shanidar cave in Iraq. Possibly the plant was used as part of some ancient funeral rite, in the same way that graves are decorated today. It has been suggested by the excavator Solecki that the plants may have been used medicinally by the Neanderthals or possibly as a stimulant to provide energy on hunting trips.

It has also been theorised as a likely herb used as the visionary "Soma" of the ancient Iranian and Indian peoples. What is known for sure is that the herb contains ephedrine and norpseudoephedrine, which are stimulants and decongestants. These constituents of the herb are useful for treating asthma, hay fever and other respiratory complaints. Like the amphetamines, ephedrine with its stimulant effect is used by people trying to lose weight and has been found in many herbal slimming remedies on sale. It is also abused by drug-users as a cheap and natural "speed". Like caffeine, however, it can make the user very "edgy" and have an adverse effect on the nerves.

As two of the herb's names suggest it can be made into an energising beverage and in this form it has been used by the Zuni Indians of New Mexico to treat the first stages of syphilis.

Morning Glory
Convolvulaceae
Ipomoea violacea/tricolour
Other names: Badoh Negro, Badungas, Blue Star, Flying Saucers, Glory Seeds, Heavenly Blue, Pearly Gates, Pearly Whites, Piule, Seeds, Summer Skies, Tlitiltzen, Wedding Bells, Yaxce'lil

The Morning Glories are many species of climbers from the Bindweed family, which bear attractive flowers and foliage. The species *I. violacea* is probably the best known and most widely cultivated. Besides being an easy to grow ornamental with showy blue and white flowers, it has been employed for thousands of years for the psychoactive properties it possesses. The whole plant contains lysergic acid amides in varying amounts with the highest concentrations found in the black or brown

seeds, There are at least twenty-eight species of Morning Glory that contain these alkaloids but the species named is the one mainly used. Particularly good varieties are Heavenly Blue, Pearly Gates and Flying

Saucers and the last-named looks very psychedelic with an eye-catching display of both blue and white patterns on its large flowers. The actual active constituents are D-isolysergic acid amide, D-lysergic acid amide (ergine), chanoclavine, clymoclavine and lysergol. The plant provides a cheap and natural substitute for LSD, although the potency is about one-tenth that of "acid". One seed contains the equivalent of one microgram of "acid" and, therefore, the dosage is anything from 100 to 300 seeds.

Shamanic use has been made of the plant by many Native American tribes such as the Aztecs, the Mayans, The Mazatecs, the Mixe and the Zapotecs and is another psychomimetic herb that has undoubtedly played a large role in shaping their culture and artistic imagery. At the tale end of the sixties, as interest in psychedelics was spreading among the "flower people", many scare-stories appeared in the media about the use of these seeds. In fact, to discourage abuse of the plant, firms that supplied seeds started to remove the name Morning Glory from their packets and catalogues and to substitute *Ipomoea*. However, this failed to fool the recreational drug-users and pyschonauts in the know.

There are various potential problems though that may be encountered because the balance of alkaloids is likely to cause unpleasant side effects like diarrhoea, nausea and vomiting, dizziness and chills. Because these effects are more difficult to rise above than the physiological effects of LSD there is the greater likelihood of a bad trip. Morning Glory can also cause miscarriage so should not be taken by pregnant women. Although overdoses on the seeds are unlikely, large amounts may be toxic and can result in shock, psychotic reactions and heart failure. People with a history of liver problems, such as hepatitis and jaundice, should also stay clear of using this plant for internal consumption.

In addition to these adverse properties the seeds of Morning Glory may be coated in pesticides or other toxins added by the seed-company to discourage abuse. Most seed packets carry a warning stating that the seeds are not for internal consumption, although this may merely mean that the seeds are considered poisonous. To be on the safe side it is best to grow your own or get them from a supplier that guarantees untreated seeds. Most gardening shops sell the seeds so it is easy enough to get the species and grow your own. It is half-hardy and usually flowers in the first year.

The alkaloids are water-soluble so one method of preparing them is to leave them soak in water for a couple of days and then to drink the liquid that the lysergic acid amides will have leached into. Another method is to chew the seeds thoroughly and to swallow them or to grind them into a powder before consumption.

The Morning Glory comes from Central America and some of the southern states but may be found growing wild as an escape in some places too, as well being commonly grown as an ornamental in parks, gardens and greenhouses worldwide.

The British rock-band Oasis had a hit album entitled (What's the Story) Morning Glory? which might well have been a reference to this plant and certainly it has often featured in both art and literature. Mary Motley, author of Devils in Waiting, has a novel simply and evocatively entitled Morning Glory and featuring an illustration of the magical herb on the cover.

The Morning Glory is ruled by Saturn and associated with the Virgin Mary and all Mother Goddesses.

Motherwort
Labiatae
Leonurus cardiaca
Other names: Common Motherwort, Lion's Ear, Lion's Tail

Motherwort is a perennial herb, which is rarely seen in gardens today. It is also a very locally distributed wild flower that grows
in waste places, on hedge banks, railway banks and at the sides of roads. The whole plant has a somewhat unpleasant smell. The leaves have a heart-shaped base and the flowers are fairly insignificant in shades of pale pink or white, looking small against the size of the leaves. It is another herb from the sage family and a very useful one too. There is an old saying, which praises its virtues very highly indeed: "Drink Motherwort and live to be a source of continuous astonishment and grief to waiting heirs". So, maybe not altogether surprisingly, it has often been referred to as "the herb of life".

Motherwort is well known as a heart tonic and a relaxant. It is a sedative by nature and also is valuable in cases of female hormonal imbalance and menopausal disorder. It is used as well for anxiety, tension and nervous problems and also for stomach problems and digestive trouble. The fresh or dried flowering herb is made into an infusion with water and an essence is made for homeopathic prescriptions. The herb contains glycosides, essential oil, bitter principles, alkaloids, acids, resin and tannin. The famous herbalist Culpeper described its action this way: "There is no better herb to take melancholy vapours from the heart, to strengthen it, and make merry, cheerful, blithe soul than this herb".

The Motherwort has a close relative from Siberia and Mexico in the form of Marihuanilla or Yi Mu Cao, *Leonurus sibiricus*, which is a similar perennial herb with sticky purple flowers. It is smoked by the Chiapas as a marijuana substitute and also used in Chinese medicine.

O

Opium Poppy
Papaveraceae
Papaver somniferum
Other names: Mawseed, White Poppy

The Opium Poppy is thought to have originated in Asia Minor but is now widespread throughout the world. It is an annual herb that can grow to 5 foot but is usually much smaller in the UK. It has large ruffled grey-green leaves and flowers of a white, lilac, red or purple colour. The whole plant exudes a milky sap or latex if broken and this juice is the source of the powerful drugs for which it is famous. Opium Poppy grows wild in many waste places, on ground that has recently been turned over and railway banks. There are many ornamental garden varieties cultivated in various shades and with colourful double flowers. These are common in parks and gardens even though the Opium Poppy contains a Class A prohibited drug.

"Opos" is Greek and means "juice". The generic name *"Papaver"* is thought to come from the Latin "papa", which translates as "breast" and the *"somniferum"* part, also from the Latin, means "sleep bearing".

It is rather aptly named as it contains very strong narcotics that, besides relieving mental or physical pain, can bring sleep and death in overdose. The Opium Poppy is the source of the following alkaloids: morphine, codeine, narcoline, narceine, thebaine, papaverine, noscapine, codamine, rhoeadine and many more that have been isolated. The narcotics in the plant are notorious for causing the problems of addiction and the word "junkie" is nowadays a household word and a modern scourge. Opium wars have been fought by the Chinese and with the British in 1839-1842, some years after Emperor Yung Cheng banned the importation of opium in 1729. Far more personal wars have been fought on a daily basis by millions of heroin and opiate addicts and by all those involved in their battle.

The Sumerians revered the poppy over three thousand years ago and the ancient Egyptians used it too. It has had a very powerful influence on the world's cultures and history as well as providing the narcotic inspiration for countless artists, composers, authors and poets. One such poet was Samuel Taylor Coleridge, who was often inspired to write his epic-style verses, such as Kubla Khan and The Ancient Mariner under "the subtle and mighty power of opium". In 1821, the author and writer Thomas de Quincey wrote Confessions of an Opium-eater about his addiction and experiences with the drug. He called himself the "Pope of the true church of opium". His addiction to the drug started when he bought a shilling's worth of laudanum in Oxford. He was transported into "an abyss of divine enjoyment". However, the enjoyment was not to last and despite many attempts at curing his addiction to opium, he died in a delerium muttering about being invited to "the great supper of Jesus Christ". Shades of the Last Supper methinks!

Charles Baudelaire took opium first while at the Sorbonne but he later went on to hashish, which is a bit of a reversal for all those who claim that Cannabis leads to harder drugs. Sometimes he mixed the two intoxicants, other times he returned to pure opium. His Reve Parisien seems likely to have been written under its influence. Another famous European writer and artist who became heavily involved with opium was Jean Cocteau. In Opium: Journal d'une desintoxication he claimed that dreams were a form of education. His bizarre drawings and strangely inspired writings reflect such an education.

The innovative author and famed ex-addict the late William Burroughs, in his work for The British Journal of Addiction vol.53, no.2 informs readers that:

"Over a period of twelve years I have used opium, smoked and taken orally (injection in the skin causes abscesses. Injection in the vein is unpleasant and perhaps dangerous), heroin injected in skin, vein, muscle, sniffed (when no needle was available), morphine, dilaudid, pantopon, eukodol, paracodine, dionine, codeine, demerol, methodone. They are all habit forming in varying degree. Nor does it make much difference how the drug is administered, smoked, sniffed, injected, taken orally, inserted in rectal suppositories, the end result will be the same: addiction".

Whatever one may think of his work or life, Burroughs is an author, who certainly tells it like it is regarding the awesome and terrible powers of opium and its derivatives. He is also responsible for having a tremendous influence on innumerable artists and writers, just like the drug opium itself has done.

The Opium Poppy features in the narrative of The Wizard of Oz, in the scene in a poppy field where Dorothy and her companions are struggling against sleep in their efforts to reach the emerald city. It certainly appears that the writers of this classic musical knew a thing or two about shamanic herbs!

The Opium Poppy and its history are covered more thoroughly in the vast amount of literature already existing about the powerful drugs the plant contains and the inspiration, as well as the misery, it has created throughout the ages.

The Opium Poppy is ruled by the Moon and has associations with very many deities including Demeter, Vulcan, Hypnos, Hades, Persephone, Pluto, Agni, Ceres and Jupiter.

P

Passion Flower
Passifloraceae
Passiflora incarnata, Passiflora caerulea
Other names: Granadilla, Maracoe, May Apple, May Pops,
Passion Vine

The Passion Flower (*P. incarnata*) is an attractive and distinctive climber found growing in most tropical countries as well as being hardy enough to survive outdoors in many parts of the Northern hemisphere, where it is often planted in parks and gardens. It originates in the southern United States of America and the West Indies.

The plant produces showy large mauve and white flowers from June to late October and these are followed by yellowish-orange fruits, which are full of seeds and a fragrant and tasty pulp. The species *P. caerulea* has blue flowers and is thought to be the hardiest of the Passion Flowers.

The Passion Flower smells like grass when burned and the dried leaves when smoked or taken as tea can produce a mild marijuana-like high. Those trying to "kick the habit" have used the herb as a tranquiliser due to its sedative and narcotic properties as well as a substitute for Tobacco. Some women have found that a tea made from half an ounce of leaves per pint of water brings relief from PMT and related problems. Passion Flower has also been employed as a remedy for neuralgia, headache, spasms and convulsions. The active ingredients are harmine and related harmala, both carboline alkaloids. These substances are MAO inhibitors, which can produce an alarming and dangerous list of symptoms when combined with a large range of drugs, foods and drink. The amounts of alkaloids in the Passion Flower are usually insufficient to cause problems but it is best to be aware of the potential dangers. A full explanation of what MAO inhibitors do and the foods and drinks to avoid, is to be found in the section on Phalaris grasses.

The fruits of many species of Passion Flower are edible and provide a tasty juice that may be drunk on its own or mixed with other fruit cordials. These fruit are increasingly showing up on the counters of greengrocers.

Pennyroyal
Labiatae
Mentha pulegium
Other names: Blechon, European Pennyroyal, Lurk-in-the-Ditch, Penny-royal, Piliolerial, Pudding Grass, Pulegium, Pulegone, Run-by-the-Ground

Pennyroyal is a perennial creeping herb from the Mint family that grows in wet soil in marshes, along streams, in moist meadows and other such watery places. There are two forms, a creeping variety, known as procumbens and a more upright form, called erecta. It is also cultivated in herb gardens. Pennyroyal is found throughout central and southern Europe and locally in southern England, becoming more rare northwards and almost absent from Scotland apart from cultivated plants. It also grows in Canada and North America. Pennyroyal is a typical Mint with whorled lilac flowers in late summer and the whole plant gives out a characteristic aroma.

It has been used in herbal medicine as a sedative and for relieving spasms, migraine and digestive disorders. It contains puligone (a yellow or green-yellow oil), essential oil, glycosides and tannin. In homeopathy Penny Royal is prescribed for asthma, coughs and arthritis. It was once used as an ingredient in an entheogenic potion drunk during the ancient Greek Eleusinian Mysteries and has been considered as a psychoactive herb by various cultures. It was recognised and burnt as an offering to the deity, Pachamana, by the shamans of Peru. In more recent times, tragic "grunge-rock" icon, the late Kurt Cobain, with his band Nirvana, wrote and performed a song called Pennyroyal Tea. Kurt suffered a chronic stomach disorder amongst other problems and this song suggests that he found some relief in this herb.

Hedeoma pulegoides, the American or Mock Pennyroyal has similar properties but a distinctly different appearance.

Pennyroyal is yet another Venusian herb.

Periwinkle
Apocynaceae
Vinca major (Greater Periwinkle), Vinca minor (Lesser Periwinkle)
Other names: Blue Buttons, Cape Periwinkle, Cat Finger, Cockles, Devil's Eye, Flower of Death, Ground Ivy, Hundred Eyes, Joy on the Ground, Old Maid, Parwynke, Pennywinkle, Perwynke, Pucellage, Sorcerer's Violet, Virgin-flower

The Periwinkles are evergreen spreading herbs that grow in woods, copses, hedge banks and shaded areas as well as being often cultivated as ornamentals and ground-cover plants in parks and gardens. The two plants look very similar apart from a difference in size and coming from different areas of the world; the Lesser comes from central Europe and western Asia, while the Greater is a native of the Mediterranean region. The flowers are formed from early spring through to mid-summer and often later. The blue flowers are very attractive against the dark green leaves.

Periwinkle is used in medicine as a diuretic, as a stimulant for cerebral conditions and for catarrh, stomach problems, colitis and diarrhoea, nosebleeds, gum disease and mouth ulcers. It has been used as an ointment to treat eczema, psoriasis and scalp irritation and also to soothe bleeding piles. It has been successfully administered to treat

vertigo, tinnitus, headache and hearing problems but the use of this herb for domestic purposes is not recommended due to potential toxic side effects.

Periwinkle contains the alkaloids vincamine, isovincamine and vincamidine and also vinblastine, vincristine, vinrosidine and vinleurosine as well as tannin, pectin and carotene.

Periwinkle has been often associated with magic and has been an ingredient in love potions as well as being regarded as a herb that wards off evil spirits and other sources of harm. It is believed that it can even protect a household if hung over the door. It has often been used in women's magical rituals and is linked strongly with the Goddess. Periwinkle is also associated with death and has been used as a funeral herb, being one plant that can be made into a wreath. Periwinkle's aphrodisiac properties extend to being credited with increasing the passion between any couple that have the herb sprinkled under their bed and of causing love to increase between them if they both eat the flowers.

Not surprisingly, Venus rules it. Periwinkle is a herb of the Mother Goddess.

Peyote
Cactaceae
Lophopora williamsii, Lophophora diffusa
Other names: Anhalonium, Anahalonium Lewinii, Echinocactus
Williamsii, Hikori, Huatari, Mescal, Mescal Buttons, Muscal Buttons,
Pellote, Peyotyl, Seni, Wakowi

No book on shamanic herbs would be complete without covering one of the most well known psychoactive plants in the world. The Peyote cactus, with its main active alkaloid mescaline, has rivalled LSD as one of the most potent mind-altering substances around. The two species named above are both true botanical oddities and grow wild in the dry, stony desert ground of Texas and Mexico but are becomingly increasingly rare and threatened with extinction due to over-collection and harvesting by unscrupulous collectors.

Peyote is one of the very few spineless varieties among some two thousand different types of cactus found growing in the world. The "Peyote button" consists of a bluish or greyish-green succulent pincushion with a tuft of furry wool-like fluff in the middle. The word "Peyote" is derived from the Nahuatl language meaning "cocoon-silk". From this central tuft emerges the pink-coloured flower, followed by the fleshy seedpod containing several tiny black seeds. The cactus grows outward and downward and as one flower goes to seed it starts to move away from the centre and goes downward to be replaced by a new one and the cycle starts again. The whole Peyote button is only a small part of the plant, which has a large carrot-like taproot underground.

The Peyote cactus is very slow growing indeed, and can take as much as thirteen years to mature. It is partially due to this long period of time necessary for its growth that it is faring so badly when collected from its wild habitat. The Native American tribes, having great reverence for the Peyote cactus, have always collected what they needed with care but sadly this has not been the case in recent years with other people who have sought out this powerful psychoactive plant. Actually, if the button is carefully cut off from the root with a wooden knife then the rootstock below should be able to clone many more button clusters

on top. These mass clusters can reach some 4 or 5 foot across and are regarded as especially powerful and sacred by the Huichol Indians. Individual plants never grow more than about four inches in diameter and increase by forming new plants at the base. The older the plants are, the more the respect that is shown for them by the Indians and these elderly cactus specimens are affectionately called "Father" or "Grandfather Peyote".

The Mexican Indians communed with their deities via the Peyote

cactus and when the Spanish conquistadors invaded the land they were not able to convince the natives that Peyote was an "evil" to be shunned. Countless Indians were horribly murdered in the name of Catholicism and the cross but the survivors incorporated elements of the Biblical imagery and belief into their own Peyote-fuelled ceremonies, and, despite all the oppression of the Spaniards, news of the cactus and its powers spread swiftly northwards to other tribes of Central America and up into the North American continent. Foremost among the Indians who spread the use of Peyote were the Mescalero Apaches and from them, by the late 1800s, it had become part and parcel of the religious practices of very many of the Plains Indian tribes. The Arapahoes, Comanche, Cheyenne, Delaware, Kiowas, Pawnees and Shawnees are all examples of Peyote-eating tribes-people.

One of the most well known Indians to be directly inspired by the Peyote cactus was the Caddo-Delaware John Wilson, who was also known as Wovoka. Wilson had been a leader in the Ghost Dance movement of the Plains Indians and had learned of the cactus and its powers from a Comanche he had met. Wovoka went into the forest with his wife and consumed as many as fifteen Peyote buttons a day for a fortnight. In the resulting Peyote intoxication and shamanic trance he was "continually translated in spirit to the sky realm where he was conducted by Peyote". He was shown the "road" leading "from Christ's grave to the Moon in the Sky, which Christ had taken in his ascent". In addition to this, Wovoka learned of many more teachings from Peyote, which were to form his pathway for the rest of his life. He was given details of ceremonies, special face-paintings that were to be worn and sacred songs that were to be sung.

Peyote is eaten raw or dried and sometimes taken brewed as a tea and is best consumed on an empty stomach. The Native American tribes who use it regard it as a "hard road" and they often have far stronger constitutions for such herbal preparations than many people around today. They also have great respect for the cactus as a sacred plant and often fast or purify themselves before rituals in which it is taken. Some tribes believe that the person who is a partaker of the Peyote cactus actually tastes his or her self. So, the purer they are, the sweeter should be the taste. Having said that, many tribes have a tribal member who for the course of a ceremony is designated "shovel man". This person is responsible for dealing with any vomiting that occurs and providing cups or can for tribal members to spit into.

One of the reasons for this problem is the very large mixture of alkaloids the cactus contains, namely at least forty -phenethylamine and isoquinoline alkaloids. Besides mescaline there is lophophorine (like strychnine in its action and can cause unpleasant side-effects besides being a respiratory stimulant), pelotine (a convulsant), anhalonine (a reflex excitant) and other alkaloids such as anhaline, anhalamine, anhalonidine, N-methylmescaline, N-acetylmescaline, O-methylanhalonidine and peyotline.

Mescaline, the main psychoactive constituent, can be extracted and isolated from the other alkaloids in the Peyote cactus or synthesised. In the form of mescaline sulphate it was to impress author and novelist Aldous Huxley so much that it became the subject matter of his book The Doors of Perception and Heaven and Hell. This book is said to have provided the inspiration for the name of the late Jim Morrison's incredibly influential rock-band The Doors. Huxley had volunteered himself as a human guinea-pig for experimentation with the drug back in 1953 and on a lovely May morning in the Los Angeles hills he cleansed the doors of his own perception. The intensity of the experience was such that he wrote:

"I became aware of a slow dance of golden lights. A little later there were sumptuous red surfaces swelling and expanding from bright nodes of energy that vibrated with a continuously changing, patterned life...The books, for example, with which my study walls were lined ...glowed, when I looked at them, with brighter colours, a profounder significance. Red books, like rubies; emerald books; books bound in agate, of aquamarine, of yellow topaz; lapis lazuli books whose colour was so intense, so intrinsically meaningful, that they seemed to be on the point of leaving the shelves to thrust themselves more insistently on my attention".

Aldous Huxley's experiences with mescaline, as well as with LSD, caused him to regard these substances as extremely beneficial, almost as means of gaining "enlightenment" and as a key to redemption for the human race. Like Timothy Leary he became a "messiah for the psyche-delic movement".

Someone else, who became very involved in this movement of the sixties, was Elizabeth Gips. Elizabeth was an author and celebrated "hippie elder". She was also the presenter of a cult "evolutionary" radio show called Changes. Her fascinating and uplifting tale is told in Scrapbook of a Haight Ashbury Pilgrim, published by Changes Press of Santa Cruz, California, and in it she says of a Peyote trip: "What a gift. The curtains waved through time, children looked like flowers on the merry-go-round in the park and licence plates on cars had cosmic meanings beyond meanings".

The religious experience that Peyote and mescaline could give to the user was, of course, as already detailed, well known to the Native American Indian tribes long before Huxley's experiments, and, indeed, became the basis for the founding of the Native American Church of North America. This church was formed by the 1906 confederation of Peyote-eating tribes and today has more than twenty five thousand members throughout America and Canada. Because Peyote forms the religious communion for the members of the church it was ruled that it was legal for these people to possess and consume the sacred cactus. The general people of America, however, have no such rights and, indeed, Peyote falls in the list of substances declared illegal by Schedule One of the Controlled Substances Act. Several American states have tried, unsuccessfully, to bring laws forbidding church members from partaking of the cactus too but they have failed in their efforts because such a law would be an unconstitutional violation of the Bill of Rights' guarantee of freedom of religion.

There is a considerable amount of evidence that shows that the

spread of Peyote-eating was a great help to the Native Americans in combating alcoholism, which many had succumbed to, partly in an effort to ease the pain of the terrible destruction that had been brought to their land and culture. Very many Indians welcomed the peaceful "love-button" Peyote cactus instead of the damaging "firewater". The Native American Peyote-users also found the cactus invaluable in treating all manner of ailments ranging from dandruff to a treatment for wounds and serious illness such as cancer. Many Indians believe that they owe their good health to a life of using Peyote as a sacrament. Even tribes who oppose its use for religious purposes grant that it is an invaluable tool in the battle against disease. Frank Takes Gun, national president of the Native American Church had this to say about the cactus:

"At fourteen, I first used Father Peyote. This was on the Crow Reservation in Montana, and I was proud to know that my people had a medicine that was God-powerful. Listen to me, Peyote does have many amazing powers. I have seen a blind boy regain his sight from taking it. Indians with ailments that hospital doctors couldn't cure have become healthy again after a Peyote meeting".

Several other cacti found throughout the Americas contain mescaline-like substances and one of these, the Doñana, is covered earlier on in this work. The San Pedro (*Trichocereus pachanoi*), the Peruvian Torch (*T. peruvianus*) and related species from the South American Andes, contain mescaline itself and are used by the people there for similar shamanic and healing properties.

Like several other psychoactive herbs covered in this book, the Peyote cactus has found its way into movie scripts and on to the big screen. In Jim Jarmusch's Dead Man, Johnny Depp stars as Blake, a young man who ends up being shot following an incident in a town he was visiting whilst seeking a job. Mortally wounded and fleeing the town, Blake is found by a Native American Indian travelling in the area. On discovering the injured man's name, the Indian rescuer decides that this Blake is the visionary English poet with the same surname. The Indian is known as Nobody and he acts as a guide and companion to the dying Blake, whom he believes is the great poet he has studied and felt a considerable affinity for. In the course of their journey, Nobody partakes of "Grandfather Peyote" and introduces his friend to it. On screen we see a vision of Depp's face transformed into a skull. The film shows how Blake becomes more and more in tune with Mother Earth and his Indian friend's ways as he dies out of his life as a white-man in a corrupt and decadent west.

Phalaris Grasses
Poaceae
Phalaris arundinacea, Phalaris canariensis, Phalaris aquatica
Other names: Canary Grass, Green Reed Grass, Reed Canary Grass, Ribbon Grass

There are two grasses found growing wild in the UK and many parts of Europe in the genus Phalaris. *Phalaris arundinacea* is very widespread growing commonly on the banks of rivers, lakes, ponds and in damp marshy places. A variegated form is grown equally commonly in many ornamental water gardens and rockeries. *Phalaris canariensis* is also grown in gardens and parks, and as the name suggests its original home is thought to be the Canary Islands and North Africa. It is this grass that is the "Canary grass".

Both these grasses and other phalaris species such as *P. aquatica* have been the focus of much debate and research in entheobotanical study circles due to the mixtures of psychoactive alkaloids they contain and these are as follows: 5-methoxy-N-methyltryptamine, 5-methoxy-N-dimethyltryptamine, DMT (dimethyltryptamine), hordenine and gramine. When extracted these substances should produce an intense, short-lasting psychedelic experience if smoked. Details of how this extraction can be done are to be found elsewhere in books such as Psychedelic Shamanism: the Cultivation, Preparation and Shamanic Use of Psychotropic Plants by Jim De Korne.

When taken internally in combination with β-carboline herbal alkaloids, like harmine from the Passion Flower, the monoamine oxidase inhibitors that these tryptamines are, will produce intense hallucinogenic effects. A definite word of caution needs to be added, however, as MAO inhibitors are very dangerous and life-threatening if consumed along with a long list of foods, drinks and other drugs. Here is a list of these incompatible substances: all foods containing trypto-phans, chocolate, cheese and dairy produce, bananas, pineapples, figs, avocados, broad beans, pickled herring, chicken liver, yeast extract,

sauerkraut, coffee, cocoa, alcohol, amphetamines, antihistamines, sedatives, narcotics, tranquillisers, ecstasy, mescaline, ephedrine, macromerine, Nutmeg, Licorice, Calamus and oil of Fennel, Dill and

Parsley. Monoamine oxidase is a vital regulator of many substances in the human body and keeps a balance. It's a bit like a chemical autoimmune system, but if it is "inhibited" then many alkaloids are activated and can produce psychedelic effects. Unfortunately for us, when a MAO inhibitor is present it can also trigger harmful effects from substances such as those in the list. Headaches, vomiting, blood pressure crises and even heart failure and death can result so it is most important not to consume any of these things for several days before and after ingesting such powerful herbal drugs. Countless tribal shamans all over the world to potentiate their sacred herbal brews such as Yage have used MAO inhibitors from plant sources. However, their rituals always include a strict period of fasting or abstinence from many foods and drinks to avoid these dangers. If using these herbs it would be wise to follow their ancient wisdom and be careful.

Phytolacca
Phytolaccaceae
Phytolacca acinosa, Phytolacca decandra, Phytolacca americana
Other names: American Nightshade, American Spinach,
Amerikanische Scharlachbeere, Bear's Grape, Branching Phytolacca,
Blitum Americanum, Coakum, Chongras, Crowberry, Garget, Herbe
de la Laque, Indian Pokeberry, Jalap, Kermesbeere, Méchoacan du
Canada, Morelle à Grappes, Pigeon Berry, Phytolacca Americana,
Phytolacca Bacca, Phytolacca Berry, Phytolaccae Radix, Phytolacca
root, Phytolaque, Phytolacca vulgaris, Pokeberry, Pokeroot, Pokeweed,
Shang-lu, Virginian Poke

The Pokeroot is found in North America, Asia, China and also in Mediterranean countries. It is such a distinctive herb that it would be very difficult to mistake the Pokeroot for any other plant. It has large leaves and grows several feet in height, with spikes of small white starry flowers at the top of the stems. These flowers are followed in turn by unusual purplish-black berries that grow all around the top of the flowering stem.

The plant is not fussy about where it grows and will even flourish in cracks in walls and concrete. If grown in a herb or ornamental garden

it may well self-seed and establish itself in other places.

The Pokeroot species *acinosa* has been used like spinach in India but the leaves need special cooking preparation techniques because they contain toxic saponines. The young shoots have also been cooked as an asparagus substitute in America, while in Portugal the juice of the berries has been employed to add colour to wines, although this has been discontinued because it spoiled the flavour. The dried herb has also been used as an adulterant to Belladonna.

The species of Phytolacca all contain phytolaccic acid, saponines and tannins as active constituents and have narcotic and purgative properties. *Phytolacca acinosa* is known as Shang-lu in China, where it is an important drug-plant. Sorcerers once used it for "seeing spirits". There are two varieties of this species, one with white flowers and root and another with red flowers and a purplish root. The former variety has been used as an edible plant but the latter type is considered too toxic. The flowers are known as Ch'anghau and are used for treating apoplexy. The root is thought to be too poisonous for internal consumption and is only administered externally.

Prairie Mimosa
Leguminosae
Desmanthus illinoensis
Other names: Prickle Weed

This plant is a hardy herbaceous perennial from North America and Canada, particularly indigenous to Illinois, as the scientific name suggests, and Dakota. It has finely divided pinnate foliage like many other members of the Pea and Bean family to which it belongs. It produces small white flowers in summer and whilst liking a lot of sun is very adaptable. The rhizome bark contains varying amounts of tryptamine alkaloids that can be used combined with herbal ß-carbolines to potentiate a "yage" or "ayahuasca" brew, as explained in a previous section.

The rare related species *Desmanthus leptolobus* is similar but smaller and not as hardy as its cousin. It has been found in Texas and grows in bare ground on poor soils and in dry places with a high lime content. Although smaller it is very invasive and rapidly colonises the area it is in. This species has proved to have even higher concentrations of alkaloids in its root-bark.

R

Rhododendron
Ericaceae
Rhododendron chrysanthum, Rhododendron caucasium/ponticum
Other names: Alpenrose, Rosebay, Snow Rose

The glossy-leaved Rhododendrons are common ornamental shrubs that are found throughout Siberia, northern Asia and other parts of the Northern Hemisphere, often growing densely on mountainsides. The species *chrysanthum* is a small bush growing to about one-and-a half feet high. This species is known as the Yellow Rhododendron, as its scientific name denotes but there are other types with white, pink and red flowers.

The leaves of Rhododendron contain a stimulant narcotic principle, which is soluble in water or alcohol. The shrub has been used in parts of Russia to treat gout, rheumatism and syphilis.

According to the nineteenth century German linguist Julius Klaproth, while travelling in the northern Caucusus at the time, he encountered a people known as the Ossetians. These Caucasian people clearly used the Rhododendron for shamanic purposes. Klaproth wrote that they "often visit ...caves to intoxicate themselves with smoke from

the *Rhododendron caucasicum*, which plunges them into sleep: the dreams that ensue are considered omens".

The Greek historian Herodotus wrote of a fruit of a tree that had psychoactive properties and was used by the Massagetae people. It has been suggested that this was the same plant. Herodotus tells us that when these people inhaled the smoke of the burning plant they were intoxicated as if by wine.

S

Saffron
Iridaceae
Crocus sativus
Other names: Alicante Saffron, Autumn Crocus, Corocus, Gatinais
Saffron, Hay Saffron, Karcom, Krokos, Spanish Saffron, Valencia
Saffron

The Saffron is a small bulbous perennial, native to Asia Minor but culti-

vated in Spain, Britain and other parts of Europe and the world. Herbalist Joseph Miller wrote: "The best Saffron in the world is grown in England being cultivated in Essex, Suffolk and Cambridgeshire". It has a flattened corm from which tufts of grass-like leaves sprout. Saffron flowers in very late summer and early autumn with rich purple blooms on short stalks. These bear three protruding bright orange stamens. It is these stamens that are the parts that are harvested and being a small part of the plant many are needed to produce any bulk quantity for commerce. This has caused the herb and spice to be a very expensive and valuable commodity. In fact it takes as much as sixty thousand flowers to yield 1 gram of the spice.

Although it is known as the autumn crocus, it is not to be confused with the similar Meadow Saffron (*Colchicum autumnale*), which has broader leaves and much lighter coloured lilac flowers. This latter species is, at times, also known by the same name.

Medicinally, Saffron has been used to treat hysteria, fevers, indigestion and cramp.

As a spice and food colouring Saffron has been used to impart colour and flavour to savouries, curries and rice dishes and for cakes and biscuits. The ancient Phoenicians made crescent moon-shaped Saffron-cakes in honour of the moon and fertility Goddess Ashtoreth. Saffron cakes are still a speciality made in Cornwall. It has a pleasant odour as well as colour. In Hebrew the word for it is "karkom" and it was an important herb and spice in Biblical times, also being used in perfume and mentioned in the Song of Solomon IV, Verse 14.

The golden dye it can be used to produce has been employed to denote royalty and high birth and robes and other garments were once dyed with Saffron. In ancient Ireland nobles and those of high birth wore a Saffron-dyed shirt called a "leincroich" as late as the 17th century.

Saffron is included here because it has been reported to have narcotic and soporific effects similar to opium. In folk magic it is believed that drinking Saffron tea helps the drinker to see into the future. It was an ingredient of some types of witches flying ointment and as is the case with many other such shamanic herbal constituents is a dangerous poison and even deadly if too much is consumed. Culpeper had this to say of the Saffron herb: "It produces a heaviness of the head and sleepiness. Some have fallen into an immediate convulsive laughter which ended in death".

Saffron is ruled by the Sun under the sign of Leo and associated with the deities Amun Ra, Ashtoreth, Eos, Indra, Jupiter and Zeus.

Saint John's Wort
Guttiferae
Hypericum perforatum

Other names: Amber, Balm of Warriors, Balm-to-the-Warrior's-Touch, Bible Flower, Cammock, Common St. John's Wort, Goat Weed, Holy Herb, Klamath Weed, Penny John, Perforated St. John's Wort, Save, Sunshine Herb, Tipton Weed, Touch-and-Heal

St. John's Wort is a common perennial herb of pastures, roadsides, hedge banks, railway banks, open woods and other grassy places. It flowers from June to August and is about 1-2 foot high and bears attractive yellow flowers with five petals. The leaves have tiny perforations, hence its specific name, and these bear the oil. It is native to Europe, Asia and North Africa and also grows in America.

St. John's Wort is used as a herbal medicine to treat menstrual disorders, gastric and intestinal problems, migraine, asthma, anaemia and for depression, anxiety and nervous ailments. It is used externally to treat painful joints and tired muscles as well as for bruises and wounds. It is a mild sedative, antidepressant and astringent in action and also stimulates intestinal secretions and bile flow. It can relieve spasms too. Its power to treat depression has resulted St. John's Wort being mass-marketed as a "natural alternative to Prozac" and millions swear by its efficacy.

Culpeper recommended the herb in this way: "A tincture of the flowers in spirit of wine, is commended against the melancholy and madness". These two afflictions of the soul are just as common today as they were in his time so it is hardly surprising that the herb is enjoying an increased popularity.

The active constituents of St. John's Wort are hypericin, resin, volatile oil and tannin. There has been some debate over whether the herb has MAO inhibiting properties but if it does, it appears that it is very mild in action. There is some danger of harmful side effects in cases of pregnancy and when breast-feeding and many manufacturers place such a caution on their brands of the herb. Oil of St. John's Wort should not be taken internally unless under medical supervision. St. John's Wort oil can cause photosensitivity and skin rashes from exposure to sunlight.

It is regarded as a herb of protection and is gathered on St. John's Day, June 24th, to be hung in bunches to ward off evil. St. John's Wort is believed to be most powerful at the time of midsummer.

It is ruled by the Sun and associated with St. John and solar deities.

Sassafras
Lauraceae
Sassafras variifolium/Sassafras officinale/Sassafras albidum
Other names: Sassafrax

The Sassafras is an aromatic deciduous tree that grows to between 20 and 50 foot in height. It is native to the eastern parts of North America and also grows in Canada. The bark of the tree varies in colour from a red or orange through to shades of brown and grey. The flowers are small and greenish-yellow and are produced in loose clusters in April and May. The leaves are either oval or lobed in shape and turn a vivid orange or red in autumn. The flowers are followed by dark blue berries,

which ripen in September.

The parts that are used are the dried leaves and also the root-bark. In Louisiana the leaves are still used in cookery to flavour soups, sauces and stews and it is the chief spice in the Cajun dish known as "gumbo file". The tea is made from the rust-brown root-bark using two table-spoons per half pint of boiling water. This tea was once so popular that it could even be bought on the streets of London. It is also known as "saloop". Sassafras was known and commonly used by the Native American tribes but it was brought to Europe by the Spanish botanist Monardes in the 16th century. The common and botanical names are said to be a corruption of the Spanish word for saxifrage. Whatever the case may be, the Spanish certainly took to this aromatic tree and once employed it in pomanders to prevent and repel the plague. Sir Francis Drake brought it into Britain.

Sassafras is a stimulant and a diuretic. It has been used to treat colds and fevers by inducing the body to perspire and it has also found favour as a herbal tonic. Herbal doctors have prescribed Sassafras to treat cases of skin eruption and for gout and rheumatic conditions. A volatile oil called safrole can be extracted and distilled from the root-bark and this has been shown to have narcotic properties.

Both MMDA (3-methoxy4, 5methylenedioxy-amphetamine) and

MDA (3,4-methylenedioxyamphetamine) can, in turn, be extracted from this oil and these substances are part of a whole group of amphetamine-related psychedelics, which include MDMA (Ecstasy), MDM, STP, PMA, TMA and DOB.

Safrole can also be synthesised from myristicin, the main psychoactive ingredient in nutmegs and mace, which although producing intense nausea and other unpleasant side effects have been indulged in by some people wishing to get high. The Sassafras tree may, however, be carcinogenic and therefore, should only be used under the supervision of a qualified herbal practitioner or taken at the consumer's own risk.

It is believed that Sassafras has the power to attract money when placed in a purse or wallet and can be added to incense burnt in the hope of gaining wealth for the would-be magician.

The planet Jupiter rules Sassafras.

Skullcap
Labiatae
Scutellaria lateriflora/Scutellaria galericulata
Other names: Blue Pimpernel, Helmet Flower, Hoodwort, Mad-dog Skullcap, Madweed, Scullcap, Virginian Skullcap

Skullcap is a perennial and hardy member of the Mint and Sage family that grows in Europe and in North America as well. It grows about 1-2 foot in height with small but attractive blue flowers from June to September. It is found in marshy places, along streams and ditches, in fens, waterlogged meadows and other such locations.

It is a sedative and excellent as a treatment for nervous disorders and insomnia. It is also anti-inflammatory in its action and is good for fevers. It has actually been used for malaria and for cases of rabies, hence its names, "Mad-dog Skullcap" and "Madweed." It contains scutellarine (a flavone glycoside). It can cause giddiness if taken in overdose and should never be combined with other tranquillisers or sedatives. Skullcap was once believed to cure infertility and it was also worn by women in the belief that this would protect their husbands from being led astray by the seductive charms of others of the "fair

sex".

Skullcap is said to have a marijuana-like effect when smoked and it can be used as an aid to relaxation and for meditation. Skullcap was utilised extensively by various tribes of Native American Indians including the Cherokee.

Skullcap is a herb ruled by Saturn.

Strawberry Tree
Ericaceae
Arbutus unedo

The Strawberry Tree is an evergreen tree that can grow to 20 foot but is usually smaller in size. It looks very attractive with a combination of white flowers and pink or red fruit amongst the dark green leaves in autumn and is ideal for ornamental gardens and shrubberies. The reddish fruit take a year to ripen so they are present at the same time as the new flowers. It is a member of the heather family and a native of southern Europe, also found in the Mediterranean areas. It grows wild in woods in Kilarney and

Bantry in Ireland and elsewhere in cultivation in parks and gardens.

The fruit of the Strawberry Tree if eaten in quantity is said to be narcotic in effect and so is the wine, which gets made in Spain and Corsica, and for this reason it is included here. However, the specific name "unedo" translates from Latin as "I eat one (only)", giving a clue to its palatability. Strawberry Tree contains arbutin.

The wood of the Strawberry Tree makes an excellent charcoal.

Syrian Rue
Zygophyllaceae
Peganum harmala
Other names: African Rue, Harmel, Rue, Wild Rue

The Syrian Rue is a perennial shrubby herb that grows wild in barren and arid places in Spain and areas of many Mediterranean countries, in Asia and the Middle East and related species are to be found in the southwestern parts of the United States and Mexico. It grows to about sixteen inches high with ferny foliage and small star-like flowers. The whole plant has a characteristic rue-like aroma, although the plant is not related in any way to its namesake the Common Rue with the botanical name of *Ruta graveolens*.

The herb, and in particular, the seeds, is rich in β-carboline alkaloids, including harmine, tetrahydroharmine, harmalol and harmaline. These alkaloids, as stated already in the sections on Phalaris grasses and the Passion Flower, are monoamine oxidase inhibitors, hallucinogenic in their action, and to be approached with caution due to adverse reactions from combining them with a long list of foods and drinks.

Harmine (7-methoxy-1-methyl-9H-pyrido [3,4-β] indole is also known as banisterine or telepathine when extracted from the psychoactive South American vine *Banisteria caapi* and as yagein when it is produced from the shamanic herb *Haemodictyon amazonicum*. Pure harmine can be isolated as harmine hydrochloride and ingested in this form by snorting, although this method may cause irritation of the nasal passages. Putting the drug on the gums and absorbing it that way can avoid this problem.

In small amounts the seeds of Syrian Rue are used as a spice and are sold commercially in marketplaces in the Mediterranean area and in Asia. The seeds have also been employed to yield a red dye used in authentic Persian rug-making, They can be burned as an incense with psychoactive properties and in India and Pakistan they are used as a narcotic. In the Hunza area of Pakistan shamans inhale the smoke given off by the burning seeds in an effort to communicate with the spirit world and its denizens. Similar uses are reported from Morocco, where they are smoked mixed in with Cannabis. In the Punjab they are also burnt at wedding celebrations.

In Indian herbal medicine the Syrian Rue herb is prescribed for asthma, as an aphrodisiac and in high doses to cause abortion. In a complete reversal of this latter-named practice, the seeds are ritually burned in a room where a new baby has just been born in parts of northwestern India and in Pakistan.

Syrian Rue is theorised to be the Vedic and Zoroastrian source of divine inspiration known as soma or haoma but Mormon Tea, Cannabis, opium and the Fly Agaric have also been put forward as candidates for this mystical shamanic brew.

Small amounts of Syrian Rue between 25 and 50 milligrams act as a mild stimulant and can cause feelings of dreaminess for a couple of hours but larger doses of about 300-750 milligrams can produce intense hallucinatory experiences. The effects vary widely from one individual to another but it is best taken internally on an empty stomach. The seeds are well chewed and then swallowed and a third of an ounce makes the usual starting dose. Depending on the user's reaction more can be taken but it is very unwise to consume more than the maximum of an ounce of seeds. The Syrian Rue has often been mixed with other psychoactive herbs such as Datura and Cannabis because the alkaloids it contains potentiate hallucinogenic effects, but as stated earlier, great care needs to be taken when combining this powerful psychoactive plant with other foods, drinks and drugs. A full list of dangerous combinations is given in the section on the Phalaris grasses.

The Syrian Rue likes a dry sandy soil and appreciates some protection from direct sun in its first year. If cultivated, it should not be moved as this may stress the plant too much and cause it to die back. It is also very susceptible to damping off, although it is very tolerant of temperature extremes. It has a reputation for being difficult to grow but the author has not encountered any problems, save for those mentioned, and at time of writing, has a three-year old pot-grown specimen growing well in ordinary garden soil, which was given no special preparation beforehand.

T

Thorn Apple
Solanaceae
Datura stramonium, Datura inoxia, Datura metel, Datura meteloides, Datura ferox
Other names: Apple of Peru, Angel's Trumpet, Devil's Apple, Downy Thorn Apple, Gabriel's Trumpet, Jamestown Weed, Jimson Weed, Sacred Datura, Stinkweed, Stramonium, Thorn-Apple, Wisakon, Yerba del Diablo

The Thorn Apple is a tall and very showy annual weed of waste places and rubbish dumps but is also found on cultivated ground at times. It grows around the world but is believed to be native to the southern states of America, Central America and Mexico and Asia. It is yet another very dangerous herb from the potato family containing tropane alkaloids. It grows to 4 foot or more with large toothed leaves, white or purple-tinged funnel-shaped flowers and spiky seedpods that look a bit like "conkers". The plant gives off an offensive smell if brushed against or lightly crushed. It flowers from summer to autumn. The thick stem can be green or a dark purplish shade. The flowers are scented and the seeds are like little black kidney beans. It is a plant that once seen is not easily forgotten.

Thorn Apple often crops up (literally!) in news stories when someone has had one appear in their garden, and not knowing what on Earth it is, they have contacted the local media. It has had a role in actual history too when it put a stop to the retreat of Mark Anthony's troops in 38 BC after they had eaten the plant as a green vegetable in error. A similar thing happened in America in the Jamestown riots of 1676 when the rebels there did likewise and became incoherent for eleven days afterwards. The name "Jimson Weed" is a corruption of Jamestown.

In more recent times Thorn Apple received a lot of publicity in books by Carlos Castaneda in which it is a "power plant", used by Yaqui Indian shamans. The first in a series of books - The Teachings of Don Juan - sparked a lot of interest in it and unwise experimentation as well, and so did Fear and Loathing in Las Vegas by the author, Hunter S. Thompson, for it is a drug mentioned several times in his novel. Writing in his first book, Castaneda informs us that after rubbing Datura as an ointment into his leg "I looked down and saw Don Juan sitting below me...I saw the dark sky above me and the clouds going by me. I jerked my body so I could look down. I saw the dark mass of the mountains. My speed was extraordinary".

Thorn Apple has been much used in witchcraft in "flying

ointments" and for other purposes and also the herb has played a major role in initiation ceremonies of various tribal peoples as well as being used for divination by many Red Indian tribes. It was used in ancient India where Sanskrit writings refer to it as "dhurstura". Further to all these uses Thorn Apple was a hallucinogen that ancient Greek priests employed as an oracle. The Chinese used it as an anaesthetic and Indian prostitutes, who knocked out their clients with it and then stole from them, even once employed it as a "Mickey Finn". It is believed that medieval gypsies brought it into Britain and Europe as herb they made use of as an intoxicant. The whole plant is psychoactive but the seeds contain the highest concentrations of alkaloids and are a serious danger to children.

In medicine, Thorn Apple has been used as a treatment for asthma, neuralgia and Parkinson's disease but it really is a very toxic plant and should never be used for domestic purposes. It contains the tropanes hyoscyamine, atropine, scopolamine and hyoscine, which are described in the section about Deadly Nightshade and Henbane. The psychedelic effects are very intense and can produce a dream state or separate reality for the user in which he or she may well believe they are in locations they are not actually in, as well as conversing with people that are not really present. For example, I once witnessed a friend under the influence of this herb, making a phone-call to someone in another country and talking to him or her, even when the phone had been disconnected! This same person intoxicated by Datura, went on to carry on a conversation with a yellow satin-jacket hanging on a nail in the wall. In the throes of Datura intoxication my friend believed the jacket to be an attractive young lady who was meditating and he went to offer her a non-existent 'joint' that he thought he was smoking. This was of particular interest, because the herb Datura, like its cousin Belladonna, is often thought of as a "femme fatale" and seems to readily link users with the dark side of the female spirit.

At another point, when a canister of scouring powder was taken out of his hand, which he was about to put to his mouth, he protested that his bottle of beer had been stolen. My friend was standing on the landing of a house but believed he was at a local bar! These situations can obviously be very dangerous indeed to an unsupervised user and the other side effects of these drugs are unpleasant in the extreme, including dryness, dizziness, confusion, diarrhoea, lack of co-ordination, babbling and slurred speech combined with amnesia to a greater or lesser degree afterwards. The user also strongly risks potential coma, convulsions and permanent damage to the heart, brain and eyesight. There is also a good chance you could end up committed to a mental institution while under its effects as well! This is another herb that is most definitely not recommended for consumption.

The Zuni, Navajo and other tribes use the species *inoxia* for shamanic purposes and this type is also known as Sacred Datura and Downy Thorn Apple. The seeds of this species are regarded as so powerful and dangerous that they are to be taken only once in a lifetime to mark an initiation. Thorn Apple is associated with the angel Gabriel and ruled by Jupiter.

Tobacco
Solanaceae
Nicotiana rustica, Nicotiana tabacum, Nicotiana glauca
Other names: Aztec Tobacco, Leaf Tobacco, Tahuaco, Tobacco Leaf, Tobacca, Wild Tobacco

Tobacco is known to everyone as the most common source of material intended for smoking purposes in cigars, cigarettes and in pipes. The wild forms of Tobacco are considerably more potent, however, and have a long history of both medicinal and shamanic use. Tobacco is yet another psychoactive herb from the Solanaceae or Nightshade family.

The species *Nicotiana tabacum* is the most widely cultivated and harvested variety and yields Virginian Tobacco. *N. rustica* is the source of a good deal of Persian Tobacco and there are very many different forms of the former species named here. *N. tabacum* can grow to some 6 foot in height with huge 18 to 24 inch pale green leaves. If the leaves are steeped in water mixed with a little soap and left for twenty-four hours the result can be used as an effective natural insecticide.

The species *N. glauca* is known as Tree Tobacco and grows as its name suggests. The Navajo Indians once employed the Tree Tobacco during Peyote rituals and at other ceremonies and meetings. As a

matter of interest, this type of Tobacco does not contain the addictive stimulant alkaloid nicotine but a very similar substance known as anabasine.

Nicotiana rustica has been long regarded as the shamanic herb par excellence and was held by some tribes to be superior even to Peyote. However, the amounts smoked by Indian shamans were far in excess of the most ardent modern chain-smoker. Shamans from tribes from the South American Orinoco River area have been known to smoke five or six huge three-foot cigars one after another and their cousins in the North had an equally ravenous appetite and tolerance for the smoke. Nicholas Monardes, a 16th century physician wrote concerning an Indian shaman's liberal use of the herb to induce a trance to divine the cause of illness in a patient. Apparently, after inhaling the Tobacco the priest "fell downe uppon the grounde, as a dedde manne, and remainyng so, accordyng to the quantitie of the smoke that he had taken, and when the hearbe hath doen his woorke, he did revive and awake, and gave theim their answeres, accordyng to the visions, and illusions whiche he sawe".

The strains of Tobacco that the Indians smoked were far more potent than the varieties harvested today and Tobacco actually contains the harmala alkaloids harman and norharman, very similar in chemical make-up to harmine and harmaline, which are known hallucinogens and covered elsewhere in this work.

Tobacco is a native of America but is now cultivated in many sub-tropical counties around the world, and on a small scale in Britain. Another species of wild Tobacco also grew in the Australian 'outback' and this type was utilised by the Aborigines living there. It is recorded by Captain Cook, that in 1770 his expedition into the Australian interior encountered native peoples who chewed a herb, (which was probably Nicotiana suavolens).

Author Richard Rudgley, in his book The Encyclopaedia of Psychoactive Substances, suggests that Tobacco was probably one of the first plants cultivated as a crop by early tribes who had been hunter-gatherers. He states that tribes-people that had an ample supply of food and other necessities for life readily available from the areas they were living in had no reason to toil away as farmers tilling the soil and yet the evidence shows that they did. Whilst the motivation for pioneering agriculture has been suggested to be a reliable source of foodstuffs at hand, Rudgley thinks that in some cases these early people took up the practice to ensure a supply of Tobacco. He holds up the Haida Indians of the Queen Charlotte Islands off the west coast of Canada and the Tlingit tribe who live on the southern coast of Alaska, as examples of tribes who practised the cultivation of Tobacco, which they habitually chewed. Before their contact with European settlers, Tobacco was the only crop they grew much of.

Medicinally, Tobacco is listed as a narcotic, sedative and emetic.

The Tobacco plant is ruled by the planet Mars.

V

Valerian
Valerianaceae
Valeriana officinalis
Other names: All-Heal, Amantilla, Baldrian, Bloody Butcher, Bouncing Bees, Capon's Tail, Cat's Valerian, English Valerian, Fu, Garden Heliotrope, Graveyard Dust, Great Wild Valerian, Herb of Witches, Phew, Phu, Phu Plant, Pretty Betsy, St. George's Herb, Setwall, Setewale, Setwell, Tobacco Root, Vandal, Vandal Root

Valerian is a perennial herb of fields, woods, hedge banks and grassy places and is often found growing in ditches and at the side of streams and other locations by water. It grows to 3 foot or more and bears clusters of pale pink flowers from June to August. It is a native of Europe and Northern Asia and is widely distributed. Valerian grows from a short rhizome with fibrous rootlets and offsets. The roots are harvested in the autumn and divided up before drying out.

Valerian is used in medicine and herbalism as a sedative and for nervous disorders as well as for headaches and to relieve spasms. It was employed in both World Wars as a treatment for shell shock. However, taken for too long a period or in overdose it can produce a state of stupor and give rise to headaches as well. Some say that it can be addictive like conventional medical tranquillisers and sedatives, so again a word of caution is deemed necessary.

In medieval times Valerian was regarded as a general panacea and often grown in monastery gardens. It was also used as a spice and in

perfume, though many people nowadays find the smell of Valerian very objectionable and hence some of its descriptive names.

Valerian has also been used in love potions as well as playing a part in voodoo magic, where the ground up root is known as "graveyard dust".

Valerian contains valeric, formic, acetic and butyric acids, camphene, pinene, valerine, chatinine, actinidine, glycosides, volatile oil and resin. Some of its constituents render it a cat psychoactive herb and in the same way as with Catmint, Kiwi fruit vines (*Actinidia* species) and other herbs with these properties, these animals love to roll around in the plants. Rats too, are reported to be attracted by its musty smell.

Valerian is ruled by Mercury and is associated with St. Bernard.

Vervain
Verbenaceae
Verbena officinalis, Verbena hastata

Other names: Brittanica, Devil's Hate, Enchanter's Plant, European Vervain, Fer Faen, Herbine, Herb of Enchantment, Herb of Grace, Herb of the Cross, Herbe Sacree, Holy Herb, Holy Vervain, Juno's Tears, Llysiaur Hudol, Lustral Water, Pigeon Grass, Pigeon's Meat, Pigeonwood, Simpler's Joy, Van Van, Verbena, Vervaine, Wizard's Plant

The Vervain is a common plant of waste ground, roadsides, railway banks and other rough grassy locations. It is a hardy perennial growing to about 3 foot high. It flowers from July to September with rather attractive small lilac flowers in spikes at the top of the long spindly stalks.

Vervain is used in herbal medicine to treat nervous problems and insomnia. Besides being an excellent tranquilliser it also has astringent and diuretic properties and can be used to treat digestive disorders, rheumatic pain and skin diseases too. It contains verbenaline, verbenine,tannin and essential oil.

Vervain has a long reputation as a healing herb and was even reputed to be a plant that grew on Mount Calvary, which was used to staunch the blood flowing from Christ's wounds. This gave it the name of "Herb of the Cross".

In magical lore Vervain has countless uses and is probably one of the most widely employed and revered herbs in the world. It is one of the three most sacred herbs of the Druids as a constituent of their "lustral water" and was used in ritual cleansings as well as a charm against ill fortune. It was also employed in divination and was gathered at the

rising of the Dog Star, Sirius, when there was no light from either sun or moon. The Chair of Taliesin bardic poem describes initiation with a drink containing this holy herb. Vervain is one of the main ingredients in the Cauldron of Cerridwen, which is the cauldron of the Celtic shape-shifter Goddess. It is a herb of inspiration and enlightenment and regarded as a powerful ally of poets and singers as well as practitioners of the magical crafts. Vervain tea can be taken to enhance clairvoyant abilities as well, and it is a herb of the visionary and the mystic.

The Romans regarded Vervain as an "altar plant" and also as a herb of protection. They further held that it was sacred to Venus the goddess of Love, and it has since been used in love spells and potions. Vervain is also believed to be a general good luck herb and a protection from evil. It is mentioned in the Holy Bible as a plant employed by King Solomon to clean and purify his temple. It was a sacred herb used by the ancient Hebrews, the Greeks and the Egyptians, and in more recent times, on the other side of the ocean, the Pawnee Indians used Vervain to improve their dreaming.

The Blue Vervain (*V. hastata*) comes from Nova Scotia and British Colombia and has similar properties to the species *officinalis*.

The Vervain is another herb ruled by Venus and associated with many deities including Diana, Isis, Cerridwen, Horus, Mars, Thor, Ra, Zeus and Aphrodite.

W

Water Lily (White)
Nymphaeaceae
Nymphaea alba
Other names: Large White Water Lily, Sweet-scented Water Lily, Sweet Water Lily, Water Nymph

The White Water Lily is a most attractive perennial plant found growing in ponds, lakes and canals throughout the UK and Europe.

There is no evidence that I can find of its use as a psychoactive herb or of its use in magic, however, it has been used medicinally and foreign water lilies have been employed by various cultures for their mind-altering properties. Possibly the White Water Lily may have similar uses. In herbal medicine it has been used as an anaphrodisiac, in other words to dampen sexual excitement and desires. It has also been

prescribed for sore throats as a gargle and for skin complaints although it is seldom used nowadays. It is a heart tonic and stimulates both the liver and spleen. The White Water Lily is astringent in its action. The harvested rootstock is the part that is used. The plant contains nymphalin, tannins and glycosides.

Species of Water Lily, probably *N. caerulea* and *N. ampla*, have often been featured in the art and mythology of the Middle and Far East and there is much to suggest that they were employed as recreational drugs, as well as in rituals. The Egyptian Blue Water Lily and the lotus of the Far East are often depicted in religious scenes and associated with deities and their corresponding priests. The lotus is a sacred plant in the Vedic religious doctrines and Hindu gods and goddesses are shown holding these lilies, emerging from them and sitting in meditation upon lotus-flower thrones. The Tibetan Buddhist tradition also features the lotus in its artwork and even in religious mantras. "Hail, the jewel in the lotus!" from one such mantra, could refer to the power of the Water Lily to transport the consumer to the abode of the gods, or of activating the pineal gland, believed to be responsible for psychic vision.

There is a school of thought that believes that the Water Lily may well have influenced much of ancient Egyptian culture. In a televised experiment shown in the series Sacred Weeds on the British Channel 4,

in the summer of '98, two volunteers took doses of the Egyptian blue Water Lily and later experienced a euphoric state, which was regarded as proof of its psychoactive properties. The flowers of the Water Lily were left to soak in wine and the infusion drunk. They later went on to eat the actual flowers and experienced further effects with no unpleasant symptoms afterwards. However, because it was an experiment only a small dose had been used and one of the points being made in a discussion after was that the Egyptians might well have taken much larger amounts.

It is also reported that in modern Mexico these water lilies are used as a recreational drug with strong hallucinatory effects. The plants contain apomorphine, nuciferine and nornuciferine, all of which are psychoactive and are probably responsible for the mind-altering properties.

The Moon rules the Water Lily.

Wild Lettuce
Compositae
Lactuca virosa (Great Lettuce), Lactuca serriola (Prickly Lettuce)
Other names: Acrid Lettuce, Green Endive, Lactucarium, Laitue
Vireuse, Lettuce Opium, Strong-scented Lettuce

Both types of Wild Lettuce grow on roadsides, railway banks, waste ground and other grassy places. They are often found growing in walls too. They are biennial plants and bloom in the second year between

July and September with very small yellow Dandelion-like flowers on tall stems. The Great Lettuce can grow up to about 5 foot high. The Prickly Lettuce is generally the smaller and spindlier looking of the two species. They are native to the UK and Europe and widely distributed, being very common in many places. The whole plant if broken yields up a white latex sap that is referred to as lettuce opium and can be collected and dried like that of the poppy.

This lettuce opium has milder narcotic and sedative properties than actual poppy opium but is used medicinally for similar purposes and smoked by recreational drug users as well for its effects. It is often also used as an adulterant to bulk up actual consignments of opium. Wild Lettuce opium contains the alkaloid lactucarium, lactucerol, latucic acid, hyoscyamine, caoutchouc, mannite and volatile oil.

The Wild Lettuce is a herb of Mars.

Woodruff
Rubiaceae
Galium odorata / Asperula odorata

Other names: Cordialis, Herb Walter, Hey Plant, Moth-herb, Muge-de-boys, Mugwet, Musk of the Woods, Star Grass, Sweet Grass, Sweet Hair-hoof, Sweet Woodruff, Wood-rova, Woodrove, Woodrowe, Woodruffe, Woodward, Wuderove

Woodruff is a hardy perennial herb that is native to northern and central Europe, North Africa and Siberia. It is a short plant reaching a maximum height of 1 foot. It likes to grow in partial shade in moist fertile soil such as that found in woods and copses. It has a creeping rhizome that throws up slender stems with star-shaped whorls of narrow leaves and clusters of white starry flowers in terminal spikes. The plant blooms between May and July. It spreads rapidly and is an excellent ground-cover plant for shrub borders and other such places. The seeds are ball-shaped and covered in hooked bristles designed to catch in the fur of passing animals and get dispersed in this way.

Woodruff, when dried, gives off a lovely aroma of newly mown grass or of hay and because of this it was much used as a strewing herb in the Middle Ages. Woodruff can be used to stuff pillows and

mattresses and legend has it that Woodruff formed the bed of the Virgin Mary. Some people, however, argue that it was actually Lady's Bedstraw (*Galium verum*). The dried herb placed in wardrobes and linen cupboards can be used to deter moths and other household pests or it can be put in between the pages of books to scent them and to discourage mustiness. The wonderful aroma is due to coumarin, a substance that occurs in several psychoactive herbs.

Woodruff has tranquillising properties and an infusion can be used to help produce a good night's sleep or to calm someone who is stressed or anxious. The tea is made using about two teaspoons of dried powdered herb to a half-pint of boiling water. Too much of it can cause vomiting and dizziness so, once again, moderation is called for. The bruised leaves have been made into poultices to treat wounds and grazes.

Gerard stated that "It is reported to be put into wine, to make a man merry and to be good for the heart and liver, it prevaileth in wounds as Cruciata and other vulnerary herbs do".

In Germany fresh sprigs of Woodruff were steeped in Rhine wine and this was known as "Maibowle". This popular intoxicating drink was traditionally imbided at Beltane or the first of May, when the celebrations mark the turning of the seasonal wheel into the start of summer.

Woodruff can be added to magical snuffs or to incenses, where it will impart its own pleasant smell and aid in fixing other perfumes.

Woodruff is a herb of Mars and linked to Goddess of the summer season.

Woolly Yarrow

Compositae

Achillea millefolium ssp. lanulosa (Nutt) Piper, Achillea lanulosa, Achillea millefolium

Other names: Mountain Yarrow, Western Yarrow, White Yarrow, Wooly Yarrow

In the section in this book covering the Dogwood it was mentioned that Woolly Yarrow has been a herb used in smoking mixtures known as "Kinnikinnick", employed by the Native American tribes, however, there is no evidence that suggests that it has any intoxicating or entheogenic properties.

Nevertheless, Yarrow stalks have found a traditional use in divination because a bundle of 50 can be used when employing the Chinese I Ching, or Book of Changes, as it is also known, to look into the future.

Yarrow species are also frequently used in herbal medicine to treat digestive problems and liver and gallbladder ailments, as well as being made into a tea as a tonic or as a remedy for colds.

Venus is the traditional planetary ruler of the Yarrow.

Wormwood
Compositae
Artemesia absinthium
Other names: Absinthe, Green Ginger, Old Woman

Wormwood is a hardy perennial herb that grows in dry conditions on banks and in waste places throughout the UK and all over Europe. It is up to about 3 foot high and flowers from July to September. Wormwood has ferny divided foliage of a greyish-green colour like most of the other Artemesias, which include the Mugwort, another useful herb. The flowers are small and a greenish-yellow. The whole plant is strongly aromatic.

It is one of the bitterest herbs known and is mentioned in the Bible for this quality where King Solomon describes the "end of a strange woman" as "bitter as Wormwood".

Wormwood's main use in herbal medicine has been to expel worms and parasites and in this role in recent years it has been used very successfully as part of Dr Hulda Clark's controversial cancer cure and parasite removal programme. She believes that her research has shown that all cancers are started by the body's reaction and attempted defence against the human liver fluke and other parasites in the presence of other pollutants and toxins in our bodies. Her findings and very detailed programme of combating the disease are covered in her book The Cure For All Cancers.

Dr Clark, writing of the herb, states "The amount you need to cure a cancer is very small, yet you cannot do without it. But the Food and Drug Administration (FDA) has regulated it as toxic! Wormwood is therefore unavailable in concentrated form from herb companies. The evidence for toxicity accepted by the FDA must have been hearsay. I have never seen a case of toxicity, not so much as a headache or nausea. The toxic level must be much higher than is needed to kill these parasites". Obviously, if she is proved correct then her findings will revolutionise beliefs about, and treatment for this killer disease.

Wormwood is also used in cases of jaundice, indigestion and lack of appetite. It is disinfectant in its action as well as a tonic and stimulant of glandular secretions. It has been used as a nervine and as a remedy for falling sickness or epilepsy. Wormwood contains thujone, thujyl alcohol, isoValerianic acid, malic acid, phellandrene, pinene, proazulene, absinthin, succine and cadinene as well as essential oil and tannin.

The thujone in it is thought to bind to the same receptor in the brain as THC, hence its mind-altering effects, although it can also have harmful effects. Native American tribes, because of the psychoactive properties that these herbs contain, smoke some related species of artemesia.

Wormwood was once used to make the liqueur drink, "absinthe", but this was made illegal because it can easily cause brain damage, paralysis and blindness. The substances in it can be very dangerous in overdose proportions, so, once again, caution is required with this herb too. Wormwood was once employed as a strewing herb and also to discourage pests like fleas and other biting insects. It has been used in magic to banish negativity. The Spanish name for A. canariensis, the species of Wormwood found in the Canary Islands, is actually "Incienso", which refers to its strong aroma like incense.

Culpeper stated that Wormwood was an excellent remedy for preventing drunkenness. He wrote that when the god Saturn met the goddess Venus and found her to be as "drunk as a hog", he exclaimed

"What, thou a fortune and be drunk? I'll give thee antipathetical cure; Take my herb Wormwood and thou shalt never get a sufiet by drinking".

The generic name "Artemesia" derives from the Greek Goddess Artemis, the Goddess of the Moon, of chastity and of childbirth. Wormwood is also linked with the deities Aesculapius, Diana, Horus, Isis and the twins, Castor and Pollux.

Wormwood is another herb ruled by Mars.

Y

Yaupon
Aquifoliaceae
Ilex vomitoria, Ilex dahoon
Other names: Black Drink Plant

The North American Cherokee and other tribes from North Carolina used this small tree from the Holly family ceremonially for the purposes of purification. As a herbal brew or "black drink" it was drunk to induce vomiting as its botanical name suggests. This practice was believed to not only purify and strengthen warriors but also to assist in producing visionary and shamanic experiences and religious ecstasies. A strong infusion was prepared from the leaves of the tree. Yaupon also has strong stimulant properties caused by the large amounts of caffeine it contains. The tree is also known as the Apalachin, Cassena and Dahoon Holly.

Yaupon is a very close relative of the South American species known as Paraguay Tea or Yerba Maté, the powdered dried leaves of which are made into a very stimulating popular beverage.

Books and Literature Consulted
in Researching this Material

Allen, Richard & Ivor Trueman (editors), Freakbeat Magazine Issue 7, Bucks, UK, 1990

Bancroft, Ann, Modern Mystics and Sages, Paladin Books, London, 1978

Burroughs, William, A William Burroughs Reader, edited by John Calder, Picador / Pan Books, London, 1982

Castaneda, Carlos, The Teachings of Don Juan, Simon & Schuster, Pocket Books, New York, 1974

Clark, Hulda Regehr, The Cure For All Cancers, New Century Press, San Diego, USA, 1993

Culpeper, N., The English Physician and Complete Herbal, Lewis and Roden, London, 1805

De Korne, Jim, Psychedelic Shamanism: The Cultivation, Preparation and Shamanic Use of Psychotropic Plants, Loompanics Unlimited, Port Townsend, WA, USA, 1994

Gerard, J., The Herball or Generall Historie of Plantes, John Norton, London, 1597

Gibson, Dan, (proprietor of the Gnostic Garden), Gnostic Garden Catalogue Issue 4, Newcastle, UK, 1998

Gips, Elizabeth, Scrapbook of a Haight Ashbury Pilgrim (Spirit, Sacraments and Sex in 1967 / 1968), Changes Press, CA, USA, 1991

Grieve F.R.H.S, Mrs M., A Modern Herbal, Tiger Books, London, 1992

Griffith, Dr. H. Winter, The Vitamin Fact File, Diamond Books, London, 1995

Huxley, Aldous, The Doors of Perception and Heaven and Hell (Flamingo Modern Classics) Lions, London, 1994

Icke, David, The Biggest Secret, Bridge of Love, Ryde, Isle of Wight, UK & Arizona, USA, 1999

Kibby, Geoffrey, An Illustrated Guide to Mushrooms and Other Fungi of Britain and Northern Europe, Parkgate Books, London, 1997,

Launett, Edmund, The Hamlyn Guide to Edible and Medicinal Plants of Britain and Northern Europe, Hamlyn, London, 1981

Lavender, Susan and Anna Franklin, Herb Craft, Capall Bann, Berks, UK, 1996

Lehane, Brendan, The Power of Plants, McGraw Hill Book Company, Maidenhead, UK, 1997

Lion Handbooks, The World's Religions, Lion Press, Oxford, UK, 1993

Marks, Howard, Mr Nice, Vintage, London, 1998

Oss, O.T. and Oeric O.N., Psilocybin: Magic Mushroom Grower's Guide, And / Or Press, Berkeley, CA, USA.

McKenna, Terence, Food of the Gods -The Search for the Original Tree of Knowledge, Ride, London, 1992

Potterton, David, Culpeper's Colour Herbal, W. Foulsham & Company, London, 1983

Rose, Gareth, The Psychedelics Volume One: An A-Z of Psychedelics, Sirius Publishing, 1993

Rose, Gareth, The Psychedelics Volume Three Psychedelic Cacti, Sirius Publishing, 1993

Rudgley, Richard, The Encyclopaedia of Psychoactive Substances, Little, Brown and Company, London, 1998

Stafford, Peter, Psychedelics Encyclopaedia, And / Or Press, Berkeley, CA, USA, 1977

Thompson, Hunter S., Fear and Loathing in Las Vegas, Vintage Books, New York, 1998

Thomson, William A.R., Healing Plants, Macmillan, London, 1978

Wasson, R.G., Soma: Divine Mushroom of Immortality, Ethnomycological Studies No. 1, Harcourt Brace Johanovich, New York, 1968

Botanical Glossary

Acrid: leaving a burning sensation in the mouth when chewed or otherwise tasted.

Agar-agar: a gelatinous substance derived from seaweed and used as a biological culture medium for bacteria, fungal spores etc.

Annual: a plant that completes its growth in one year.

Anthers: the part of the stamen containing pollen.

Aromatic: having a more or less agreeable odour.

Auriculate: with ear-like lobes (usually small) at the base.

Alternate: staggered singly around a stem.

Axil: upper angle between a leaf or bract and a stem.

Berry: a soft fruit containing the seeds in pulp.

Bi-ennial: a plant that completes its growth in two years, usually flowering in the second.

Bract: a leaf-like organ, often coloured, supporting a flower.

Bulb: a bulb is more or less globular and consists of fleshy scales or modified leaves. It is often underground.

Catkin: cylindrical male or female infloresecence of trees and shrubs such as the hazel and willow.

Corolla: the petals of a flower considered as a whole.

Deciduous: falling off, usually of a plant, tree or shrub that loses its leaves in autumn.

Entheobotanical: pertaining to the study of sacramental plants and those used for shamanic purposes.

Flowerhead: an arrangement of flowers in a group, often surrounded by rows of bracts.

Hermaphrodite: possessing functional male and female reproductive organs.

Inflorescence: flower cluster including the stem, flowers and bracts.

Invasive: having a tendency to invade or encroach upon new land.

Lanceolate: lance-shaped.

Latex: a white or yellow milky sap.

Ovate: egg-shaped.

Perennial: a plant that lives for more than two years and flowers each year.

Rhizome: underground stem, usually perennial.

Rib: the central part or vein of a leaf

Semi-aquatic: growing partially in water, amphibious in nature.

Spadix: a spike of flowers.

Stamen: the male reproductive part of a flower bearing pollen.

Umbel: an inflorescence with all the flower stalks arising from a single main point. The outer flowers open first.

Glossary of Medical Terms

Abortifacient: induces abortions.

Acid: the opposite to an alkali, having a sour taste and the ability to neutralise alkalis as well as having potential corrosive properties.

Addiction: psychological or physiological dependence on a drug or other substance.

Adrenal gland: gland found next to the kidney producing adrenaline and several steroid hormones.

Adulterant: substance that makes another impure when mixed, often used to add to the bulk.

Alkali: a chemical substance that neutralises and is neutralised by acids.

Alkaloid: a nitrogen-containing constituent of a plant or herb, usually with potent medicinal or pharmacological properties.

Allergy: excessive sensitivity to a substance.

Amenorrhoea : abnormal absence of menstruation.

Amine: a naturally occurring body chemical produced in response to emotion, fear and exercise.

Amino acid: an organic acid and a constituent of protein. It is derived from ammonia.

Ammonia: a colourless gas with a pungent smell and alkaline properties.

Amphetamine: a synthetic stimulant and decongestant drug.

Anaemia: too few healthy red blood cells or too little haemoglobin in these cells.

Anaesthetic: used to deaden pain.

Angina (angina pectoris): chest pain with sensation of impending death.

Anorexia (anorexia nervosa): absence of appetite, an associated eating disorder.

Antacid: neutralises acid.

Anti-bacterial: destroys bacteria or inhibits their growth.

Antibiotic: inhibits growth of germs or kills them.

Antidote: a medicine taken to counteract a poison.

Anthelmintic: a worm-killer.

Antihistamine: prevents histamine, a body chemical which dilates the smallest blood vessels, constricts the muscle surrounding bronchial tubes and stimulates stomach secretions.

Anti-oxidant: prevents oxidation (combining with oxygen).

Antiseptic: prevents or inhibits the growth of germs.

Aphrodisiac: arouses or enhances instinctive sexual desires.

Aromatic: with a spicy fragrance and stimulant properties.

Artery: blood vessel that carries blood away from the heart.

Asthma: disease of the respiratory system, characterised by wheezing and breathing difficulty. It is caused by bronchial spasms and may be an allergic reaction to various stimuli or caused by other factors.

Astringent: shrinks tissues and prevents the secretions of fluids.

Bacteria: microscopic germs that differ from viruses. Some bacteria are beneficial to health and others cause disease.

Bitters: medicine or tonic with a bitter flavour.

Bronchitis: inflammation of the breathing tubes in the chest.

Carcinogen: a substance able to cause cancer.

Cardiac: pertaining to the heart.

Catarrh: inflammation of the mucous membranes of nose and throat.

Cerebral: of the brain.

Chorea: St.Vitus's Dance, a degenerative disease of the nervous system.

Chronic: a disease of long-standing.

Conjunctivitis: inflammation of the outer membrane of the eye.

Contraceptive: prevents pregnancy.

Consumption: another name for tuberculosis or 'wasting disease.'

Convulsion: violent uncontrollable spasm.

Cyanogenic glycoside: sugar that can be used to produce the toxin cyanide.

Cystitis: inflammation of the urinary system and bladder.

Decongestant: a drug that relieves congestion, especially of the respiratory system.

Delerium: mental disturbance with hallucinations, agitation and incoherence.

Dermatitis: skin inflammation or irritation.

Digestive: pertaining to the digestion.

Diuretic: causes increased flow of urine.

Dosage: amount of a medicine to be taken for a specific complaint or amount of a substance required for an effect.

Dropsy: disease in which watery fluid accumulates in the cavities and tissues of the body.

Eczema: non-contagious skin disease, often with redness, irritation and scaling. It may be allergic in origin.

Emaciation: state of extreme leanness, wasting away.

Emetic: causes vomiting.

Emphysema: a disease of the lungs.

Enteritis: disease of the intestines.

Epilepsy: symptom or disease characterised by brain disturbance causing convulsions and loss of consciousness.

Essential oils: the same as volatile oils. Such oils evaporate at room temperature.

Expectorant: removes secretions from the bronchial tubes.

Extract: solution prepared by soaking the herb in solvent and then evaporating the solution to concentrate it.

Fatigue: weariness after exertion, a general reduction of the efficiency of the body and its organs.

Flatulence: distension of the stomach and intestines due to accumulation of gases.

Gastritis: inflammation of the stomach.

Gingivitis: gum disease.

Gland: group of specialised cells that manufacture and secrete materials not required for their own needs.

Glycoside: a chemical compound that yields sugar and other substances by hydrolysis.

Gout: disease characterised by inflammation of the joints, especially the big toe.

Haemoglobin: iron-based pigment necessary for the transportation of oxygen by the red blood cells.

Haemorrhage: excessive bleeding.

Hallucinogen: produces hallucinations - apparent sensual experiences that do not exist for other people.

Hepatic: pertaining to the liver.

Herb: plant valued for its medicinal qualities or for its aroma or taste.

Histamine: body chemical that causes tissue constriction and dilates small blood vessels. This can lead to leakage of fluid to form a rash or irritation.

Homeopathy: practice of introducing minute doses of a substance to cause the same symptoms as a disease that is being treated. Homeopaths acknowledge no diseases, only the symptoms in the body.

Hormone: chemical substance produced by the endocrine glands - the thymus, pituitary, thyroid, parathyroid, adrenal, ovaries, testicles and pancreas. These substances regulate body functions and maintain balance.

Hydrolysis: decomposition by a chemical reaction with water.

Hyperacidity: excessive acid, especially of the stomach.

Hypertension: high blood pressure.

Hypnotic: producing sleep.

Hypotension: low blood pressure.

Hysteria: state of uncontrolled excessive excitement, a neurotic condition with possible anaesthesia and convulsions.

Insecticide: kills insects.

Irritant: causes irritation.

Impotence: lack of ability of a male to achieve or maintain erection of the penis.

Insomnia: inability to sleep.

Jaundice: symptomatic disease of the liver, due to damage to the organ, obstruction of bile production or destruction of red blood cells. It is characterised by yellowing of the skin and whites of the eyes.

Laryngitis: inflammation of the larynx, the cavity in the throat containing the vocal chords.

Laxative: a substance that stimulates bowel movements.

Libido: sex drive.

Lymph glands: glands located in the lymph vessels of the body. These glands act to trap foreign and infectious material.

Mania: mental derangement with excessive excitement and possible violence.

Metabolism: chemical and physical processes in the maintenance of life of the body.

Mg.: abbreviation for milligram, one-thousandth of a gram.

Migraine: periodic severe headaches, possibly accompanied by visual disturbance, nausea, vomiting and sensitivity to light.

Monoamine oxidase: an enzyme, which assists in the breakdown of amines in the body.

Monoamine oxidase inhibitor: a substance that blocks the action of monoamine oxidase and may give rise to adverse effects. A monoamine oxidase inhibitor may also block the action of other vital enzymes.

Mucilage: gelatinous substance containing protein.

Narcotic: drug or substance that produces stupor and deadens pain. Narcotics tend to be addictive. They act by depressing the central nervous system and producing both drowsiness and euphoria.

Nervine: a drug that helps restore the nerves to a healthy state.

Neuralgia: intense intermittent pain caused by inflammation of the nerves of face and head.

Ophthalmic: of the eye, pertaining to conditions of the eye.

Oxidation: combining a substance with oxygen.

Parasite: an animal or plant drawing nutriment directly from another species of life.

Pelvis: basin-like cavity in the area of the kidneys.

Parkinson's Disease: a progressive degenerative disease of the nervous system with tremor, muscular rigidity and emaciation.

Pharyngitis: inflammatory disease of the pharynx or throat.

Poultice: material held between cloth or muslin to provide heat and moisture to an area of the body's surface. Poultices contain an active substance and a base to hold it together. They are applied when hot and removed when cool.

Prostate: gland in the male surrounding the neck of the bladder and urethra. In older men it has a tendency to become infected, obstructed or cancerous.

Psoriasis: chronic skin disease with patches of red flaking skin.

Psychedelic: expanding the mind's awareness.

Psychoactive: affecting the mental state.

Psychonaut: a voyager into the mind's capabilities, an explorer of the mind, possibly with the aid of hallucinogenic drugs or other shamanic practices. Just as an astronaut explores 'outer space' a psychonaut does the same for 'inner space.'

Psychosis: mental disorder with altered reality states or personality changes for the sufferer, often with hallucinations and delusions.

Pulmonary: of the lungs.

Purgative: a powerful laxative.

Pyelitis: inflammation of the renal pelvis.

Relaxant: a substance, which calms and relaxes, similar in action to a tranquiliser.

Renal: of the kidneys.

Resin: a complex chemical substance that is usually hard, transparent or translucent in nature and which can cause effects in the body.

Saponin: chemicals found in plants that may cause toxic reactions. Saponins often produce soapy lathers with water.

Sedative: reduces anxiety and aids sleep.

Stimulant: stimulates activity of organs of the body. Stimulants produce short-term energy.

Stomachic: promotes contraction of the stomach muscles.

Sudorific: produces copious sweating.

Syphilis: a contagious venereal disease.

Tannins: complex acidic mixtures of chemicals found in plants.

Terpenes: complex hydrocarbons. Most volatile oils are terpenes.

Tincture: solution of chemicals in an alcoholic solvent.

Tinnitus: a ringing in the ears.

Tonic: medicinal preparation to promote and restore well-being.

Toxin: a poison.

Tranquiliser: a substance that reduces anxiety and calms a person who is disturbed.

Tryptophan: a certain type of amino acid.

Tyramine: a chemical component of the body, which at normal levels helps maintain a healthy blood pressure. In the presence of some drugs, such as monoamine-oxidase inhibitors, tyramine can rise to levels that can be toxic or even fatal.

Virus: infectious organism that reproduces itself within the cells of an infected host.

Volatile oils: see Essential oils.

Water-soluble: dissolves in water.

Index

Absinthe 133
Achillea lanulosa 37, 132
Achillea millefolium 132
Aconite 28, 76
Aconitum napellus 76
Acore 16
Acorus Calamus 16
Acrid Lettuce 128
Actinidia 124
Adonis autumnalis 50
Aesculapius 135
African Rue 114
Agaricineae 41
Agni 86
Ajuga reptans 12
Alicante Saffron 105
All Heal 73
All-Heal 122
Alpenrose 104
Alpinia officinarum (Hance) 46
Alraun 70
Amanita muscaria 41
Amanita pantherina 44
Amantilla 122
Amber 108
American Bittersweet 10
American Mandrake 71
American Nightshade 101
American Spinach 101
Amerikanische Scharlachbeere 101
Amun Ra 108
Anahalonium Lewinii 92

Anaphalis margaritacea 37
Anethum graveolens 40
Angel's Trumpet 116
Anhalonium 92
Anthony, Mark 117
Anthropomorphon 70
Aphrodite 126
Apocynaceae 90
Apollo 41, 75
Apple of Peru 116
Aquifoliaceae 135
Aquilegia vulgaris 29
Araceae 16
Arberry 7
Arbutus unedo 113
Arctium lappa 13
Arctostaphylos uva-ursi 7
Aristolochiaceae 5
Artemesia absinthium 133
Artemesia vulgaris 41
Artemis 33
Asafetida 4, 5
Asafoetida 4
Asarabacca 5, 6
Asarum europaeum 5
Ashes 20
Ashtoreth 107
Asperula odorata 130
Asthma Weed 62
Athene 51
Atropa Belladonna 33, 34
Atropos 33, 34, 36
Autumn Crocus 105

Ayahuasca 104
Aztec Tobacco 119

B
Baaras 70
Bacchus 26
Bach 16
Bad Man's Oatmeal 51
Badoh Negro   79
Badungas 79
Balder 75
Baldrian 122
Balm of Warriors 108
Balm-to-the-Warrior's-Touch 108
Banewort 33
Bardana 13
Bardona 13
Basam 11
Baudelaire, Charles 85
Bazzies 13
Bear's Foot 49
Bear's Grape 7, 101
Bearberry 7, 37
Beaver Poison   51
Beer Flower 55
Beggar's Buttons 13
Beggart 44
Beggary 44
Belene 53
Belladonna 14, 28, 33, 103
Bellona 36
Betonica officinalis 53
Betony 53
Bhang 20
Bible Flower 108
Big Laughing Gym 8, 9

Big Laughing Jim 8
Birdlime 73
Birdlime Mistletoe 73
Bisom 11
Bittersweet 9, 10, 11, 34
Bizzom 11
Black 33
Black Cherry   33
Black Drink Plant 135
Black Nightshade 53
Bladderpod 62
Blechon 88
Blitum Americanum 101
Blodeuwedd 14
Bloody Butcher 122
Blow 20
Blue Buttons 90
Blue Pimpernel 111
Blue Star 79
Blue Vervain 125
Boo 20
Bouncing Bees 122
Brain Thief 70
Branching Phytolacca 101
Breeam 11
Brighid 57
Brittanica 124
Broccoli 20
Brodswort 53
Broom (Scotch) 11
Browme11
Brum 11
Buddha sticks bush 20
Bugleweed 12, 13
Bunk 51
Burdock 13, 14

Burren Myrtle 7

Burroughs, William 86

Buttercup (Meadow) 15, 16

C

Cactaceae 37, 92

Calamus 6, 16, 17, 18, 19,100

California Poppy 19, 20

Caltha palustris 16

Cambuck 51

Cammock 108

Campanulaceae 62

Canary Grass 99

Canary Island Broom 12

Caniculata 53

Cannabinaceae 20, 55

Cannabis 20, 21, 22, 23, 24, 25, 26,
55

Cannabis indica 20, 22

Cannabis ruderalis 20

Cannabis sativa 20, 22

Cape Periwinkle 90

Capon's Tail 122

Carum petroselinum 28

Cassilago 53

Cassilata 53

Castaneda, Carlos 117

Castor 135

Cat Finger 90

Cat-lye 53

Cat-mint 26, 124

Cat's Delight 26

Cat's Valerian 122

Cat's Wort 26

Catarrh Root 46

Catnep 26

Catnip 26

Catrup 26

Celastrus scandens 10

Cerberus 78

Ceres 86

Cerridwen 75, 126

Charge 20

Chariot of Venus 76

Charras 20

Chenile 53

Cherry 33

China Root 46

Chongras 101

Christmas Flower 49

Christmas Herb 49

Christmas Rose 49

Cinnamon Sedge 16

Cinquefoil 27, 28, 29

Circe 36

Circejium 70

Circoea 70

Circuta virosa 28

Clark, Dr Hulda 133

Claviceps purpurea 38

Clavicipitaceae 38

Clite 13

Clog-weed 13

Clot-Bur 13

Cloud Burr 13

Coakum 101

Cobain, Kurt 90

Cockle Buttons 13

Cockle-bur plant 13

Cockles 90

Cocteau, Jean 85

Colchicum autumnale 107

Coleridge, Samuel Taylor 85
Colic Root 46
Columbine 29
Common Motherwort 82
Common Reed 31
Common St. John's Wort 108
Compositae 13, 47, 132, 133
Conium 51
Conium maculatum 51
Convolvulaceae 79
Cordialis 130
Cornaceae 36
Cornus sanguinea 36
Cornus stolonifera 36
Corocus 105
Cortinariaceae 8
Corydalis 31, 45
Corydalis cava 31
Coryphantha macromeris 37
Cowbane 28
Crampweed 27
Creeping Cinquefoil 27
Crocus sativus 105
Crowberry 101
Cuckold Buttons 13
Cuckoo Button 13
Culpeper 11, 53, 55, 83, 109, 134
Culverwort 29
Cupid's Car 76
Cupressaceae 58
Cytisus scoparius 11

D
Daft-berries 33
Dagga 20
Damiana 32

Datura ferox116
Datura inoxia 116
Datura metel 116
Datura meteloides 116
Datura stramonium 116
Deadly Dwale 33
Deadly Nightshade 10, 33, 34, 35,
    36, 43, 57, 70
Death's Head 41
Death's Herb 33
DeKorne, Jim 99
Demeter 86
Desmanthus illinoensis 103
Desmanthus leptolobus 104
Depp, Johnny 98
De Quincey, Thomas 85
Deus Caballinus 53
Devil's Apple   116
Devil's Berries 33
Devil's Cherries 33
Devil's Dung 4
Devil's Eye 90
Devil's Fuge 73
Devil's Hate 124
Devil's Herb 33
Diana 33, 126, 135
Digitalis purpurea 12
Dill 40, 41
Dionysus 36
Divale 33
DMT 43, 99
Dogberry 7
Dog-piss 53
Dogwood 36, 37, 132
Dollwort 70
Doñana 37, 38, 98

Donkeys 13
Donnerbesen 73
Dope 20
Downy Thorn Apple 116
Dragon-doll 70
Druids 74, 124
Dry high 20
Dulcamara 9
Dumbledore's Delight 76
Dwale 33
Dwaleberry 33
Dway Berry 33

E
Earth Smoke 44
East India Root 46
Echinocactus Williamsii 92
Eddick 13
Edible Burdock 13
Egyptian Blue Water Lily 128
Enchanter's Plant 124
Enebro 58
English Valerian 122
Eos 108
Ephedra equisetina, Bunge. 78
Ephedra gerardiana 78
Ephedra nevadensis 78
Ephedra sinica, Stapf. 78
Ephedra viridis 78
Ephedraceae 78
Ephedrine 78
Ergot 38, 39
Ericaceae 7, 60, 104
Eschscholzia californica 19
Essenes 66
European Pennyroyal 88

European Vervain 124
Eyebright 62

F
Fair Lady 33, 34
Felonwood 9
Felonwort 9
Fenkel 40
Fennel 40, 41, 52, 100
Fer Faen 124
Ferny Plant 40
Ferula foetida 4
Fetter-grass 49
Fetterwort 49
Field Balm 26
Finkle 40
Five finger blossom 27
Five Fingers 27
Five-leaf-grass 27
Fivefinger 27
Flag Root 16
Flapper-bags 13
Flores Tiliae 61
Flower of Death 90
Fly Agaric 41, 42, 43, 61
Flying Saucers 79, 80
Foeniculum vulgare 40
Food of the Gods 4
Fox, James 44
Fox's Clote 13
Foxgloves 12
Freakbeat 65
Freya 75
Friar's Cap 76
Friar's Cowl 76
Frigga 75

Fu 122
Fumaria Indica 44, 45
Fumaria officinalis 44
Fumariaceae 31, 44
Fumiterry 44
Fumitory 44, 45
Fumus 44
Fumus Terrae 44
Funny stuff 20

G
Gabriel 119
Gabriel's Trumpet 116
Gage 20
Gagroot 62
Galanga 46
Galangal 46, 47
Galenmannchen 70
Galium odorata 130
Galium verum 131
Gallows 70
Gallow's-man 70
Gallowgrass 20
Ganeb 20
Ganesha 20, 33
Ganga 20
Garden Heliotrope 122
Gargaut 46
Garget 101
Gatinais Saffron 105
Gemeiner Wacholder 58
Genevrier 58
Genista canariensis 12
Gerard 55
Giggles-smoke 20
Ginepro 58

Ginseng 71
Gipsyweed 12
Gips, Elizabeth 96
Gipsywort 12
Gladdon 16
Glory Seeds 79
Gnetaceae 78
Goat Weed 108
God's Fingers and Thumbs 44
Gold 20
Gold Cup 15
Golden Bough 73
Goof butt 20
Goose Tansy 27
Goosegrass 27
Graminaceae 31
Granadilla 87
Granny's Bonnets 29
Grass 20
Graveyard Dust 122
Great Burdock 13
Great Lettuce 128
Great Morel 34
Great Wild Valerian 122
Greater Periwinkle 90
Greek avenging Furies 59
Green Broom 11
Green Endive 128
Green Ginger 133
Green Reed Grass 99
Grenouillette 15
Griefo 20
Grieve, Mrs M. 58
Griffo 20
Ground Ivy 90
Guazza 20

Gum Asafetida 4
Guttiferae 108
Gymnopilus junonius 8
Gymnopilus spectabilis 8
Gypsy Comb 13

H
Hades 75, 86
Happy Major 13
Hardock 13
Haret Hogeurt 47
Harmel 114
Hash 20
Hashish 20
Hawaiian 20
Hawkweed 47
Hay 20
Haymaker's Mushroom 67
Hay Saffron 105
Hazel-wort 5
Heavenly Blue 79, 80
Hebenon 53
Hecate 36, 51, 53, 78
Hecklow 51
Hedeoma pulegoides 90
Hellebore 49, 51
Hellebore (Black) 49
Hellebore (Green) 50
Hellebore (False) 50
Hellebore (White) 50
Helleborus niger 49
Helmet Flower 76
Hemleac 51
Hemlic 51
Hemlock 28, 51, 52, 53
Hemp 20

Henbane 53, 54, 57, 70
Henbell 53
Herb 20
Herb of Circe 70
Herb of Enchantment 124
Herb of Grace 124
Herb of the Cross 124
Herb of Witches 122
Herb Walter 130
Herbe de la Croix 73
Herbe de la Laque 101
Herbe Sacree 124
Herbine 124
Hexenmannchen 70
Hey Plant 130
Hieracium pilosella 47
Hikori 92
Hill, John MD 45
Hing 4
Hofmann, Albert 39
Hog-bean 53
Hog's Bean 53
Holy Herb 108, 124
Holy Vervain 124
Holy Wood 73
Hombrecitos 64
Hooch 20
Hoodwort 111
Hops 55, 56, 57
Houseleek 29
Horse Saver 58
Horus 126, 135
Huatari 92
Humlock 51
Humulus lupulus 55
Hundred Eyes 90

Hurr-burr 13
Huxley, Aldous 95, 96
Hylic 51
Hyoscyamus 53
Hyoscyamus niger 53
Hypericum perforatum 108
Hypnos 86

I
Icke, David 66
Ilex dahoon 135
Ilex vomitoria 135
Indian hay 20
Indian hemp 20
Indian Pokeberry 101
India Root 46
Indian Tobacco 62
Indra 108
Ipomoea violacea/tricolour 79
Iridaceae 105
Isana 53
Isis 126, 135

J
Jagger, Mick 44
Jalap 101
James's Tea 60
Jamestown Weed 116
Japanese Belladonna 57, 58
Jesus 73, 85
Jimson Weed 116
J jay jive joint 20
Jointfir 78
Joy on the Ground 90
Juanita Weed 20
Juniper 58, 59

Juniperus communis 58
Juno's Tears 124
Jupiter 29, 45, 62, 75, 86, 108, 111
Jupiter's Bean 53
Jusquiasmus 53

K
Kaempferia galanga 46
Kaif 20
Kandaharre Hing 5
Kaphnos 44
Kapnos 44
Karcom 105
Kauii 20
Kava-Kava 16
Keckies 51
Kermesbeere 101
Kex 51
Kif 20
King's Coach 76
Kinnikinnick 7, 36
Kisses 13
Klamath Weed 108
Krokos 105

L
Labiatae 12, 26, 82, 88
Labrador Tea 60, 61
Lactuca serriola (Prickly Lettuce)
    128
Lactuca virosa (Great Lettuce)
    128
Lactucarium 128, 130
Lady's Bedstraw 131
Lady's Lockets 44
Ladykins 70

Laitue Vireuse 128

Lamb's Bread 20

Large White Water Lily 126

Las Mujercitos ("the little
women") 64

Laughing Jim 8

Laughing Mushroom 8

Lauraceae 109

Lawnmowers Mushroom 67

Leaf of Delusion 20

Leaf Tobacco 119

Ledum groenlandicum 60

Ledum hypoleucum 60

Ledum latifolium 60, 61

Ledum palustre 60

Leguminosae 11, 103

Leary, Timothy 96

Leo 44, 108

Leonurus cardiaca 82

Leonurus sibiricus 83

Lesser Galangal 46

Lesser Periwinkle 90

Leto 57

Lettuce Opium 128

Liberty Caps 64, 65, 67, 68

Lignum Crucis 73

Lime (Common) 61

Lime (Large-leaved) 61

Lime (Small-leaved) 61

Linden Flowers 61

Linn Flowers 61

Lion's Ear 82

Lion's Herb 29

Lion's Tail 82

Llysiaur Hudol 124

Loaves of Bread 53

Lobelia 62, 63

Lobelia (Blue-flowered) 62

Lobelia inflata 62

Locoweed 20

Lophophora diffusa 92

Lophopora williamsii 92

Loppy Major 13

Loranthaceae 73

Los Ninos ("the children") 64

Love Leaves 13

Love Weed 20

LSD 38, 66, 81, 92, 96

Lurk-in-the-Ditch 88

Lustral Water 124

Lycopus virginicus 12

M

Ma Huang 78

Mach 20

Mad-dog Skullcap 111

Madweed 111

Magical Blend (magazine) 65

Magic Mushroom Band 64-65

Magic Mushrooms 64, 65, 66, 67

Marjoram 29

Mandragen 70

Mandragor 70

Mandragora 70

Mandragora autumnalis 70

Mandragora officinalis
/officinarum 70

Mandrake 70, 71, 72, 73

Manicon 34

Mannikin 70

MAO inhibitor 38, 88, 99, 100

Mao-ken 15

Maraba 46
Maracoe 87
Marihuanilla 83
Marijuana 20, 22, 23, 24
Marks, Howard 23
Marley, Bob 24
Mars 6, 8, 16, 47, 57, 59, 122, 126, 130, 132, 135
Marsh Cistus 60
Marsh Marigold 16
Marsh Tea 60
Mary Werner 20
Maryjane 20
Mauii 20
Mawseed 84
May Apple 71, 87
May Pops 87
McKenna, Terence 65
Mealberry 7
Méchoacan du Canada 101
Mekilwort 34
Melampode 49
Melmot Berry 58
Mentha pulegium 88
Mercury 11, 41, 44, 73, 124
Mescal 92
Mescal Buttons 92
Mescaline 92, 95, 96, 98
Mex 20
Mexican 20
Mexican Damiana 32
Mezz 20
Miller, Joseph 55, 106
Misseltoe 73
Mistletoe 73, 74, 75
Moanague 7

Mohammed, Prophet 76
Mohasky 20
Monardes, Nicholas 121
Monkshood 76, 77, 78
Moon 19, 86, 128
Moor Grass 27
Morabaceae 55
Morelle à Grappes 101
Morrison, Jim 95
Mormon Tea 78, 79
Morning Glory 79, 80, 81, 82
Mota 20
Moth-herb 130
Mother Goddess 29, 91
Motherwort 82, 83
Motley, Mary 82
Mountain Box 7
Mountain Yarrow
Mountain Yew 58
Mouse-ear 47
Mouse-ear Hawkweed 47, 49
Mu 20
Muge-de-boys 130
Muggle 20
Mugwet 130
Mugwort 41. 133
Murderer's Berry 34
Muscal Buttons 92
Mushrooms 64
Musk of the Woods 130
Musquash Root 51
Mutah 20
Myristica fragrans 40
Myrtle Grass 16
Mystyldene 73

N

Naughty Man's Cherries 34
Nepeta cataria 26
Nettles 29
Nicotiana glauca 119
Nicotiana rustica 119, 121
Nicotiana tabacum 119
Nidor 44
Nip 26
Nirvana (band) 90
Noble Princess of the Waters 64
Nutmeg 40, 100
Nymphaea alba 126
Nymphaea ampla 127
Nymphaea caerulea 127
Nymphaeaceae 126

O

Oasis (band) 82
Odin 75
Oeric, O.N. 69
Old Maid 90
Old Wife's Hood 76
Old Woman 133
Opium Poppy 84, 85, 86
Origanum vulgare 29
Oss. O.T. 69

P

Pan 26, 31, 59
Panaeolus foenisecii 67
Panaeolus sphinctrinus 67
Paneolus subalteatus 68
Panther Cap 44
Papaver somniferum 84
Papaveraceae 19, 31, 84

Papilionaceae 11
Parkinson's disease 32
Parsley 28
Parwynke 90
Passiflora caerulea 87
Passiflora incarnata 87
Passifloraceae 87
Passion Flower 87, 88
Passion Vine 87
Pearly Everlasting 37
Pearly Gates 79, 80
Pearly Whites 79
Peganum harmala 114
Pellote 92
Penny John 108
Penny-royal 88
Pennyroyal 88, 89, 90
Pennywinkle 90
Pentaphyllon 27
Perforated St. John's Wort 108
Periwinkle 90, 91
Persephone 86
Personata 13
Peruvian Torch 98
Perwynke 90
Peyote 92, 93, 94, 95, 96, 97, 98,
   121
Peyotyl 92
Phalaris aquatica 99
Phalaris arundinacea 99
Phalaris canariensis 99
Phalaris Grasses 99
Phew 122
Phragmites australis 31
Phu 122
Phu Plant 122

Phytolacca 101, 102, 103
Phytolacca acinosa 101
Phytolacca americana 101
Phytolacca Bacca 101
Phytolacca Berry 101
Phytolacca decandra 101
Phytolacca root 101
Phytolacca vulgaris 101
Phytolaccaceae 101
Phytolaccae Radix 101
Phytolaque 101
Pig's Rhubarb 13
Pigeon Berry 101
Pigeon Grass 124
Pigeon's Meat 124
Pigeonwood 124
Piliolerial 88
Pilosella 47
Piper methysticum 16
Piule 79
Pliny 72
Pluto 8, 86
Poaceae 99
Pod 20
Podophyllum peltatum 71
Poison Hemlock 51
Poison Parsley 51
Poison Tobacco 53
Pokeberry 101
Pokeroot 101
Pokeweed 101
Pollux 135
Porsch 60
Pot 20
Potentilla reptans 27
Prairie Mimosa 103

Pretty Betsy 122
Priapus 26
Prickle Weed 103
Prickly Lettuce 128
Psilocybe caerulescens 69
Psilocybe caerulipes 69
Psilocybe cyanescens 70
Psilocybe lanceolata 64
Psilocybe mexicana 66
Psilocybin Mushrooms 64, 65, 67
Pucellage 90
Pudding Grass 88
Pukeweed 62
Pulegium 88
Pulegone 88
Pythagoras 71

Q
Queen Mother of Poisons 76

R
Ra 31, 126
Raccon Berry 70
Randall, Robert 23
Ranunculaceae 15, 29, 49, 76
Ranunculus acris 15
Rapuntium inflatum 62
Rastafarians 24
Rat Root 16
Red 20
Red Bearberry 7
Red Willow 36
Reed Canary Grass 99
Reefer 20
Rhododendron 104
Rhododendron caucasium

/ponticum 104, 105
Rhododendron chrysanthum 104
Ribbon Grass 99
Roach 20
Rockberry 7
Roeg, Nicholas 44
Rope 20
Rosaceae 27
Rosebay 104
Rose, Gareth 15
Rubiaceae 130
Rudgley, Richard 121
Rue 114
Run-by-the-Ground 88
Russian Belladonna 57

S
Sacred Datura 116
Saffron 105, 106, 107
Sagackhomi 7
Saint John's Wort 108
San Pedro 98
Sassafras 109, 110, 111
Sassafras albidum 109
Sassafras officinale 109
Sassafras variifolium 109
Sassafrax 109
Sativa 20
Saturn 5, 26, 49, 51, 53, 55
Save 108
Scarlet Berry 9
Scheiteregi 44
Scilaminae 46
Scopoli, Giovanni 57
Scopolia carniolica 57

Scopolia japonica 57
Scopolia lutescens 57
Scopolia parviflora 57
Scopolia tangutica 57
Scotch Broom 12
Scullcap 111
Scutellaria galericulata 111
Scutellaria lateriflora 111
Seaside 40
Seeds 79
Semihomo 70
Sempervivum tectorum 29
Seni 92
Setewale 122
Setwall 122
Setwell 122
Shamen, The (band) 65
Shang-lu 101
She-To 64
Shit 20
Shrooms 64
Shui-lang 15
Simpler's Joy 124
Sinsemilla 20
Skinny 20
Skullcap 111, 112, 113
Sleeping Nightshade 34
Sleepy Nightshade 34
Smoke 20
Smoke snop 20
Snow Rose 104
Socrates 52
Solanaceae 9, 33, 53, 57, 70, 119
Solanum Dulcamara 9, 34
Soma 79
Sorcerer's Berry 34

Sorcerer's Root 70
Sorcerer's Violet 90
Sorceror's Cherry 34
Spanish Broom 11
Spanish Saffron105
Spartium junceum 12
Spliff 20
Splim 20
Spotted Corobane 51
Spotted Hemlock 51
St. Bernard 124
St. Dunstan 76
St. George's Herb 122
St. James's Tea 60
St. John 109
St. John's Wort 108
Star Grass 130
Stick 20
Sticky Jacks 13
Stinking Roger 53
Stinkweed 20, 116
Stoned 23
Storm Hat 76
Stramonium 116
Straw 20
Strawberry Tree 113
Strong-scented Lettuce 128
Stropharia cubensis 69
Strophariaceae 64
Stuff 20
Summer Skies 79
Sumpfporsch 60
Sun 31, 59, 75, 108, 109
Sunkfield 27
Sunshine Herb 108
Super Furry Animals 23

Sweet Bugle 12
Sweet Cane 16
Sweet Fennel 40
Sweet Flag 16
Sweet Grass 130
Sweet Hair-hoof 130
Sweet Lucy 20
Sweet Myrtle 16
Sweet Root 16
Sweet Rush 16
Sweet Sedge 16
Sweet Water Lily 126
Sweet Woodruff 130
Sweet-scented Water Lily126
Sweethearts 13
Symphonica 53
Synkefoyle 27
Syrian Rue 114

T
Tahuaco 119
Taubenkropp 44
Taxus brevifolia 37
Tea 20
Teamster's Tea 78
Texas Tea 21
Thai sticks 21
Theophrastus 72
The Woodpecker of Mars 41
Thompson, Hunter, S 117
Thor 126
Thorn Apple 57, 70, 116, 117, 118, 119
Thorn-Apple 116
Thorny Burr 13
Thunderbesem 73

Thyme 29
Thymus vulgaris 29
Tilia platyphyllos 61
Tiliaceae 61
Tillieul 61, 62
Tipton Weed 108
Tlitiltzen 79
Tobacca 119
Tobacco 119, 120, 121,122
Tobacco Leaf 119
Tobacco Root 122
Tooth-wort 53
Touch-and-Heal 108
Touch-me-not 13
Trichocereus pachanoi 98
Trichocereus peruvianus 98
Turkey Burrseed 13
Turnera aphrodisiaca 32
Turnera diffusa 32
Turneraceae 32
Turner, William 72
Tuzzy-muzzy 13
Twist 21

U
Umbelliferae 40, 51
Upland Cranberry 7
Upright Meadow Crowfoot 15
Urticaceae 55
Uva-ursi 7

V
Valencia Saffron 105
Valerian 122
Valeriana officinalis 122
Valerianaceae 122

Van Van 124
Vandal 122
Vandal Root 122
Vapour 44
Venus 14, 27, 30, 75, 91, 125, 134
Veratrum album 50
Veratrum viride 50
Verbena 124
Verbena hastata 124
Verbena officinalis 124
Verbenaceae 124
Vervain 41, 124
Vervaine 124
Vesta 26
Vinca major 90
Vinca minor 90
Violet Bloom 9
Viper's Weed 21
Virgil 75
Virgin Mary 82, 131
Virgin-flower 90
Virginian Poke 101
Virginian Skullcap
Viscum album 73
Vishnu 33
Vomitwort 62
Vulcan 86

W
Wacky baccy 21
Wakowi 92
Waraitake 8
Wasson, R. Gordon 42
Water Bugle 12
Water Horehound 12
Water Lily (White) 126

Water Nymph 126
Water Parsley 51
Wax Dolls 44
Waxwork 10
Wedding Bells 79
Weed 21
Western Yarrow 132
Whacky baccy 21
Wheat 21
White Poppy 84
White Yarrow   132
Wild Fennel 40
Wild Ginger 5
Wild Lemon 70
Wild Lettuce 128, 130
Wild Nard 5
Wild Rhubarb 13
Wild Rosemary 60
Wild Rosmarin 60
Wild Rue 114
Wild Tobacco 119
Wisakon 116
Witches Berry 34
Witches Broom 73
Witches Mannikin 70
Wizard's Plant 124
Wolf's Bane 76
WoMandrake 70

Wood of the Cross 73
Wood-rova 130
Woodrove 130
Woodrowe 130
Woodruff 130, 131, 132
Woodruffe 130
Woodward 130
Woody Nightshade 9, 34
Woolly Yarrow 132
Wooly Yarrow 37, 132
Wormwood 133, 134
Wovoka 94
Wuderove 130

Y
Yaqui Indian shamans 117
Yaupon 135, 136
Yaxce'lil 79
Yerba 21
Yerba del Diablo 116
Yerba Maté 136
Yew 37

Z
Zeus 33, 108, 126
Zingaberaceae 46
Zygophyllace 114

BOOKS

O is a symbol of the world, of oneness and unity. In different cultures it also means the "eye," symbolizing knowledge and insight. We aim to publish books that are accessible, constructive and that challenge accepted opinion, both that of academia and the "moral majority."

Our books are available in all good English language bookstores worldwide. If you don't see the book on the shelves ask the bookstore to order it for you, quoting the ISBN number and title. Alternatively you can order online (all major online retail sites carry our titles) or contact the distributor in the relevant country, listed on the copyright page.

See our website www.o-books.net for a full list of over 500 titles, growing by 100 a year.

And tune in to myspiritradio.com for our book review radio show, hosted by June-Elleni Laine, where you can listen to the authors discussing their books.

MySpiritRadio